For Barbara
with love from
Peter

May 1954

HE WROTE TREASURE ISLAND

al mio caro amico
H. Walter Barnett, questo ricordo
di Samoa Girolamo Pieri-Nerli offre

Portrait of Robert Louis Stevenson
from a drawing by Count Nerli

HE WROTE
TREASURE ISLAND

The Story of Robert Louis Stevenson

by

G. B. Stern

Illustrated with photographs and
line drawings

WILLIAM HEINEMANN LTD
MELBOURNE :: LONDON :: TORONTO

FIRST PUBLISHED 1954

PRINTED IN GREAT BRITAIN
AT THE WINDMILL PRESS
KINGSWOOD, SURREY

ACKNOWLEDGMENTS

The Author and Publishers acknowledge with thanks the kind permission of Messrs. W. & R. Chambers Ltd. to quote passages beginning on pp. 25, 26, 57 from Rosaline Masson's *I Can Remember Robert Louis Stevenson* and of Messrs. Hodder & Stoughton Ltd. to quote passages beginning on pp. 164, 165, 166 from J. M. Barrie's *Margaret Ogilvie*. They also wish to thank the editor of Collins *Young Elizabethan* for permission to use material from an article on Robert Louis Stevenson which the Author wrote for that magazine.

ILLUSTRATIONS

CHAPTER ONE

"DEAR Cousin Maggie; I don't know what to say but I'll tell you a story"—and we may be sure that Maggie enjoyed her Cousin Lou's story even more than a letter, because it was all about pirates and illustrated by the author. Unluckily, once she had read it she probably threw it away; you can't be expected to keep all the letters that all your cousins wrote you, after you'd read them once and they weren't properly printed in a book. But it happened that the little boy who made up this tale for her about pirates was one day, about twenty-five years later, to write another story of buccaneers, and it was called *Treasure Island*.

Robert Louis Stevenson was a delicate only child who lived in a gloomy house in Edinburgh, where he was almost too carefully looked after and wrapped up and cherished by his mother and father and Cummy, his nurse, who all adored him and thought no more wonderful bairn had ever been born in Scotland nor in the whole world. You can't escape from being a bit spoilt if everything is against you like that, but Smout, as his father always called him (which means 'little salmon') was a hundred times happier when he could be set free from all that coddling on his frequent visits to his grandfather, the Rev. Lewis Balfour, at the Manse at Colinton; where, up to a few years ago, the strong wooden gates at the entrance were still peppered with shot-holes from being used as a target in those days by Lou and his cousins. There were always a troop of cousins for him to play with; he actually had fifty first cousins, forty of them on the Balfour side, though it was improbable he would find them all staying there at the same time. No less than five were called Lewis after their grandfather, so they had to have nicknames to distinguish them, taken from the places where they were born—Delhi Lewis, for instance, and Poona Lewis and Cramond Lewis. Delicate as he was, one might have expected Lou to shrink timidly from this troop of strong rough older children, but on the contrary, he was the wildest of hooligans, and ringleader in all their games of high adventure.

2

It was an exciting sort of garden belonging to the Manse; a sunny slope of lawn ran downhill from the kirkyard—"we were full of homely Scottish superstitions of grues and ghosts and goblins." . . . The black still water of the burn naturally offered the children every sort of chance to get into serious trouble, with its deep mill-pond and islands not to be reached without difficulty and danger—though that was hardly likely to stop them:

"I remember climbing down one day to a place where we discovered an island of this treacherous material. O the great discovery! On we leapt in a moment, but on feeling the wet, sluicy island flatten out into a level with the river, and the brown water gathering about our feet, we were off it again as quickly. It was a 'quicksand' we said."

Most of the girls and boys who looked forward to their holidays at the Manse, lived to be much older than Lou, and when they were eighty, still remembered and chuckled at his romantic ideas for their entertainment, and the daring expeditions that so often ended in disaster.

Then all the horns were blown in town;
And, to the ramparts clanging down,
All the giants leaped to horse
And charged behind us through the gorse.

On we rode, the others and I,
Over the mountains blue, and by
The Silver River, the sounding sea,
And the robber woods of Tartary.

A thousand miles we galloped fast,
And down the witches' lane we passed,
And rode amain, with brandished sword,
Up to the middle, through the ford.

The intrepid "others and I" nevertheless stood somewhat in awe of the silvery-haired old minister who was their grandfather; Lou remembers, a little while before the old man died, seeing him given a dose of Gregory Powder and then a barley-sugar drop to take the taste away (and the evil smell, too, of that horrible gritty mixture); but when his aunt wished to give one of the drops to Lou, the rigid old gentleman interfered: "No Gregory mixture, no barley-sugar," said he.

All the same, none of the children's escapades

4

seemed to end in scoldings or punishments; perhaps Aunt Jane saw to that; Miss Jane Balfour, mentioned by her beloved Lou in gratitude as 'chief of our aunts' in *A Child's Garden of Verses*, a collection of poems much more fun to read than any of us would imagine from its rather sloppy title; Stevenson's second thoughts were rarely better than his first; he had originally meant to call them *Penny Whistles*, and should have stuck to it.

All his life, forty-four years and one month, Robert Louis Stevenson never lost his zest for high adventure on land and sea, seeking it out when it failed to seek *him* out (but it usually did). At Colinton Manse, except when he simply had to stay in bed with fever and coughing, he couldn't bear to be out of the fun of dressing up and acting at being anybody and everybody except himself. Above all, he played soldiers with such furious enthusiasm, galloping horses, handling ships in storms, slaying dragons and bivouacking in the shrubbery, that he was nearly always exhausted by the evening:

"Once as I lay, playing hunter, hid in a thick laurel, and with a toy gun upon my arm, I worked

5

myself so hotly into the spirit of my play, that I think I can still see the herd of antelope come sweeping down the lawn and round the deodar; it was almost a vision."

Asked what he was doing, he replied: "Ah'm just hunting blaauwboks." Again, one warm summer evening on the front green, his aunt showed him the wing-bone of an albatross, and told him of its largeness and how it slept upon the wing above the vast Pacific.

Of course it cannot always have been fine weather and life out-of-doors for young Smout; so naturally we picture the little boy who scribbled down pirate stories for his dear Cousin Maggie, as always likely to be hiding himself away on wet days, absorbed in a book; but to tell the astonishing truth, he was not able to read for himself till he was eight; Cummy must have been to blame for this, and his father and mother; why bother to learn if you can always find somebody willing to read aloud to you by the hour? And then one warm evening he and Etta had been playing together, and presently he was sent off into the village on an errand, something prompted him to take a book of fairy-tales and go down through a fir wood, *reading* as he walked; he said that he never forgot the shock of that pleasure: "for it was then that I knew I loved reading". Another time, it must have been shortly afterwards, when he was absorbed in a fat old volume called *The Arabian Nights Entertainment*, his clergyman grandfather came in behind him; the Rev. Lewis Balfour was 'a man we counted pretty stiff,' so Lou was terrified: "But instead of ordering the book away, he said he envied me."

Funny, all the same, that already two years before this glorious discovery of a world of books into which he could plunge alone and unaided, he should be dictating to his mother that *History of Moses* for which their Uncle David had offered a prize among his nephews and nieces. Seeing so vividly in his mind what the Seven Plagues of Egypt must have been like, Lou made them far more horrible than when we just see the words 'seven plagues' written down; almost as horrible as they must have been in reality; and then he drew a picture of the Israelites going out of Egypt, marching along wearing tall hats, yellow trousers, some with bundles on their shoulders like Dick Whittington, some leading camels with long noses and thin legs, and Moses himself smoking a pipe.

He was really quite good at drawing. Look at his comic woodcuts for Moral Emblems! A fussy critic might protest that the little boy's idea of the costume of the Israelites from the Book of Exodus was not quite orthodox. But Cummy saw to it that her bairn could have passed a pretty stiff exam on the Old Testament long before he could even spell out words of one syllable.

When he was not at the Manse with his cousins, he was rather a lonely little boy, except for those grown-ups to whom he was the precious only child; his pretty gay mother had French blood in her, and could romp with him as though she herself were a child; yet it was his father whom he loved best of all, who used to take him on his knee and tell him of adventures, sometimes grim, always thrilling, of shipwrecks and great breakers and tall lighthouses and the wild clans who had lived in the heather, and of outlaws and their hiding places. Cummy, too, was another born story-teller, and he kept her at it in a lordly manner and with all the tyranny that we think is our right when we are small and ill and can't sleep; and therefore on the many long feverish

8

nights when he simply couldn't get off, he would order her to read to him from the Bible. When he woke in the morning and imperiously demanded she should read to him again, she would pretend that he still wanted the Bible; but he, no longer in fear of the darkness, the bogles and the howling of the wind round the house in that bleak northern city, frankly preferred his story-books by Ballantyne: "Why, Cummy, it's daylight now!"

She sometimes varied Ballantyne with his favourite Robinson Crusoe; or with the Pilgrim's Progress; or with her tales of the brave Covenanters who had been persecuted for their faith; he also confesses with amusement, later on, that in his tender childhood a favourite author of both himself and Cummy was the Rev. Robert Murray M'Cheyne, and especially a line of that gentleman's verse which charmed him, though he had not the remotest idea what it was about:

"Jehovah Tschidkenu is nothing to her".

One of the nicest things about Robert Louis Stevenson was that he never forgot to be grateful to people and to let them know it in letters and dedications and poems, realising that silent gratitude isn't very much use to anyone who has done a lot for you. Certainly he remained grateful to Cummy all his life for her tireless care and affection, and acknowledges it in his dedication to *A Child's Garden of Verses*:

> For the long nights you lay awake
> And watched for my unworthy sake:
> For your most comfortable hand
> That led me through the uneven land;
> For all the story-books you read:
> For all the pains you comforted:
> . . . From the sick child, now well and old,
> Take, nurse, the little book you hold.

In another poem called 'Escape at Bedtime', he tells us—but we could easily have guessed it—how he enjoyed tip-toeing downstairs and outside the house in Heriot Row for a spot of illicit star-gazing:

> They saw me at last and they chased me with
>   cries,
> And they soon had me packed into bed;
> But the glory kept shining and bright in my eyes,
> And the stars going round in my head.

When you have finished reading the whole life of Robert Louis Stevenson, you will agree that it goes on being very much what he has described in that one verse.

Whatever games Lou played, he acted with all his might—like the cow in yet another of his poems: 'She gives me cream with all her might, to eat with apple tart'. Usually he dressed up and *lived* the part so as to forget he was not really, for instance, a gallant soldier fighting against desperate odds at the Siege of Sebastapol in the Crimean War—which was undoubtedly the immediate result of his Aunt Jane giving him a toy sword for his birthday: not a 'toy' as Cummy would have wished; but a rather heavy weapon, considering his size and lack of sturdiness. Seeing that he was flushed and coughing, and it was raw foggy weather, they (the usual 'they') insisted, in spite of his indignant struggles and protests, on wrapping him up tightly in a huge shawl. "Do you think it will look like a night march?" he asked, unwillingly giving in at last. People were always trying to swathe him in shawls whenever he was really enjoying himself; 'Velvet Coat' was to be his nickname in Edinburgh when he was a young man; and years later an old lady who had known him on the island of Samoa, said that a replica of that garment by now so well-known was always over his wife's arm, while she anxiously followed him round to lay it over his shoulders.

Few writers have ever described sword-play with the zest and excitement of Stevenson; not just swinging and slashing and using a lot of words, but with that far more important quality in a writer, of knowing exactly what he was talking about. He never lost his keen boyish delight in weapons, for he must have been twenty-nine when he showed another little boy, his stepson Lloyd Osbourne, how the ordinary slender 'walking-stick' he carried about with him was in reality a heavy steel bludgeon. R.L.S. recommended it warmly as a weapon for use in a tight place, because it couldn't go off like a pistol and was not nearly as hard to get swiftly into action as a sword-stick.

He remarked once that he loved fighting, but all the same hated people to be angry with him— "the uncomfortable effect of fighting," he said, shrewdly laying his finger on the weak spot; yet his love of fighting was a long way off from truculence and bullying for its own sake; always he fought for the oppressed; at instances of cruelty or injustice he would flare up in a moment, and the flames raged until even if he failed, he had at least done his utmost in a lost cause and against heavy odds. Do you remember that thrilling fight in *Kidnapped*, when Alan Breck and David Balfour defended themselves in the round-house of the brig *Covenant* against the crew of fifteen?—

"Alan, leaping back to get his distance, ran upon the others like a bull, roaring as he went. They broke before him like water, turning and running, and falling one against another in their haste. The sword in his hand flashed like quicksilver into the huddle of our fleeing enemies. . . . 'And O, Man,' he cried in a kind of ecstasy, 'Am I no a bonny fighter?' "

There are such throngs of stories revealing Stevenson's passion for soldiers that one hardly knows which to choose. A friend has described a dinner-party where 'the meal was endlessly prolonged while General Stevenson marched his troops between the mustard-pot and the salt-box, and dashed out to crush a flanking-party from behind a dish of olives'. He must have been over thirty when Mrs. Fleeming Jenkin, wife of the

Professor who had been his severe tutor in engineering at the University, happened to enter their schoolroom quietly, when her young son of fourteen and R.L.S. were both lying flat on the floor, engaged in some terrific miniature campaign; hearing her step, Louis looked up and cried hotly: "Look here, it's not fair! What am I to do when he keeps *on* undermining my earthworks?"

The same indulgent Aunt Jane who gave him the sword, also brought him his first large box of wooden soldiers. Shall we hear what he had to say about it in his own words? They always make a thing sound so much more real:

"After dinner, on the first day of new acquisition, I was told to exhibit my soldiers to grandpapa. The idea of this great and alarming dignitary stooping to examine my toys was a new one; and I ranged my wooden militia with excessive care upon the broad mahogany, while my grandfather took his usual nuts and port wine. Not only was he pleased to approve of the way in which I had marshalled my array, but he also gave a new light to me on the subject of playing with soldiers —a technical term, you observe. He told me to

Toy soldier which belonged to R.L.S. and is
now in the possession of the author

Three of the stamps from the R.L.S. memorial issue

make the battle of Coburg. Now Waterloo I knew, and the Crimean battlefields I knew (for they were within my memory) but this Coburg was a new and grand idea, a novel vista of entertainment, an addition to my vocabulary of warlike sports; and so I have never forgotten it."

He could hardly have had a more martial birthplace than Edinburgh, where morning and evening the garrison bugle was blown from the castle walls. His stepdaughter Belle Osbourne (a grand old lady who has lately died at the age of ninety-five) can remember how homesick he had been for Edinburgh during those last years when (another form of that endless putting-to-bed)—his health made him a permanent exile on an island in the Pacific:

"More than once he talked to me of the Calton Hill and how he would love to hear again the bugle at nine o'clock from the castle."

Of course, all the years when for various reasons he could not get away from Edinburgh, he had longed and longed for travel to far

15

places; but all the same he was a Scotsman to the core and proud of belonging there, proud of his nationality no less than he was proud of belonging to the family of Lighthouse Stevensons.

CHAPTER TWO

LOUIS' ancestors and kinsmen would undoubtedly have been surprised to hear that
their profession seems to us at all romantic; what
would be romantic, they might have asked in
broad Scots, about their title: Engineers to the
Board of Northern Lights? They were widely
known as the Lighthouse Stevensons; and Robert
Stevenson, the founder of the firm, was responsible for ringing round the dangerous coast
of Scotland with twenty tall towers built under
his supervision. He also invented suspension
bridges hung on chains; you can see a fine one
across the Firth of Forth, and another spanning a
broad chasm from Bristol across to Clifton.
Perhaps we should travel a little further back and
speak of this Robert Stevenson's stepfather,
Thomas Smith, whom our young Louis used to
call 'the lamp and oil man', not to deride him,
but in admiration for his vigorous achievements,
for not only was he ship-owner and underwriter
and a merchant burgess of Edinburgh, but sole

owner of a company of tinsmiths, coppersmiths, brass-founders, blacksmiths and japanners, and had designed a system of oil lights in place of coal fires. This same Robert Stevenson, if you are interested in lighthouses (and which of us is not?) will be chiefly and for ever famous for having built the Bell Rock Lighthouse on a sunken reef eleven miles out to sea from Arbroath. The Bell Rock, or Inchcape, was covered over twelve feet at every tide, a menace to all good sailors. There was a poem which most children were taught to recite about fifty years ago, called 'The Inchcape Rock', about a good and thoughtful Abbot of Aberbrothock who hung a bell on the rock to warn mariners that they were drawing near; the bell was cut away by the wicked Sir Ralph the Rover, and years afterwards, with uncanny justice, he was wrecked on that very rock:

> But even in his dying fear
> One dreadful sound could the Rover hear,
> A sound as if with the Inchcape bell
> The devil below was ringing his knell.

At last Robert Stevenson's attention was drawn to the danger of the Bell Rock by a 74-gun ship,

H.M.S. *Tork*, going down in a gale with all hands on board. His grandson, our Robert Louis Stevenson, wrote a family chronicle called *Records of a Family of Engineers*, and boys who are especially keen on such things as engineering and light-houses will probably find these records of what can be done while beset by every difficulty of storm and gale and tide, a hundred times more interesting than any made-up story, more exciting even than *Treasure Island*. Louis wrote a poem, too, where he movingly expresses his sadness that he himself had been too frail in health to follow in the line of succession:

> Say not of me that weakly I declined
> The labours of my sires, and fled the sea;
> The towers we founded and the lamps we lit,
> To play at home with paper like a child.

The artist Turner has painted a glorious picture of the Bell Rock Lighthouse, threshed by waves mountain-high; they can hardly have been as high when Sir Walter Scott was rowed out in a small boat to see the edifice, and wrote in their album a few lines of tribute which R.L.S. must have read with throbbing pride when his father,

Thomas Stevenson, Robert's son, took him on a tour of inspection aboard the little steamer *Faroes*, round all their lighthouses. For Thomas was another notable Lighthouse Stevenson, and invented the system of intermittent revolving light still in use all over the world.

Sir Walter Scott, as you may imagine, was Louis' hero. When he wrote from Samoa to salute his younger Scottish 'pen friend', J. M. Barrie, saying: "And now there are two of us that the Shirra would have patted on the head," he was still far from realising how famous he had himself become as the author of *Treasure Island* and *Kidnapped* and *Jekyll and Hyde* and *The Master of Ballantrae*. Shirra means Sheriff; Scott had once been Sheriff of Edinburgh, and both Stevenson and Barrie were students of Edinburgh University.

From the moment lighthouses were mentioned, we seem to have been jumping to and fro in time and place; but they kept on haunting Louis, and we find them looming up again and again all through his life; when he was married to Fanny Osbourne, and Thomas Stevenson gave her a house at Bournemouth, Louis at once called it 'Skerryvore' after the lighthouse built by his father and his Uncle Alan, ten miles south-west of Tyree:

"The name of my house here in Bournemouth is stolen from one of the sea-towers of the Hebrides which are our pyramids and monuments."

Lighthouses and islands and the sea, soldiers and swords and ships, mills and rivers, all of these were sure to claim Louis' full and absorbed attention when he was a boy and when he grew up; yet he had other loves, and one of them was the theatre, though again we would be wrong to imagine from his passion for everything to do with the stage that he was himself to write a good play; he did write a few plays, but they were astonishingly bad; the dramatic scenes in his books were excellent, but that may well have been because he was not trying so hard to produce something actable. How it would have thrilled him could he have known that one day, nearly a hundred years after he was born, *Treasure Island* was performed on the real stage, and then turned into a film; and *Kidnapped* presented on the television screen, bagpipes and all, with a truly magnificent Alan Breck.

By chance it was a ship that piloted him into becoming the happy owner of all those bold melodramas which he put on in his toy theatre; because whenever he was on his way to see the ships, down the wide street which links the city of Edinburgh with the sea, he would stop and look in at the window of a stationer's shop where there was a small model theatre displayed in working order, with slides of 'a forest set', 'a combat', and 'robbers carousing'. . . . And all round were hung sheets of just the sort of plays that any boy might buy had he enough pocket money, for they cost no more than a penny plain and tuppence coloured. Here is the stirring roll-call of those which at different times he had somehow managed to acquire for his own: *Aladdin*, *The Red Rover*, *The Blind Boy*, *The Old Oak Chest*, *The Wood Daemon*, *Jack Sheppard*, *The Miller and his Men*, *The Smuggler*, *The Forest of Bondy*, *Robin Hood*, *The Waterman*, *Richard I*, *My Poll and my Partner Joe*, *The Inchcape Bell* (imperfect), and *Three-Fingered Jack, the Terror of Jamaica*. When he was not manipulating the little cardboard figures in these bloodthirsty dramas, he would take his paint-box and colour those which the difference of a penny had left plain; indeed, he asserts defiantly, that he would not stoop to 'tuppence coloured' and forego the pleasure of messing about with crimson lake and Prussian blue and gamboge and green.

The same zest in dressing-up for dark and sinister pretences, made him leader of a group of boys who started meeting toward the end of their summer holidays in North Berwick, on evenings when the night was already black; each with a tin bull's-eye lantern buckled to the waist on a cricket belt under their buttoned topcoats, so that no one should be aware, when they sallied forth, that they were the Lantern Bearers. The gangster games which some boys nowadays copy from bad films, have nothing on those night sorties as later described by their 'inventor':

"Toward the end of September, when school-time was drawing near and the nights were already black, we would begin to sally from our respective villas, each equipped with a tin bull's-eye lantern. ... . We wore them buckled to the waist upon a cricket-belt, and over them, such was the rigour of the game, a buttoned topcoat. They smelled noisomely of blistered tin; they never burned aright, though they would always burn our fingers; their use was naught; the pleasure of them merely fanciful; and yet a boy with a bull's-eye lantern under his topcoat asked for nothing more. The fishermen used lanterns about their boats, and it was from them, I suppose, that we had got the hint; but theirs were not bull's-eyes, nor did we ever play at being fishermen. The police carried them at their belts, and we had plainly copied them in that; yet we did not pretend to be policemen. Burglars, indeed, we may have had some haunting thoughts of; and we had certainly an eye to past ages when lanterns were more common, and to certain story-books in which we had found them to figure very largely. But take it for all in all . . . to be a boy with a bull's-eye lantern under his top-coat was good enough for us.

When two of these asses met, there would be an anxious 'Have you got your lantern?' and a gratified 'Yes!' That was the shibboleth, and very needful too; for as it was the rule to keep our glory contained, none could recognise a lantern-bearer, unless (like the pole-cat) by the smell. Four or five would sometimes climb into the belly of a ten-foot lugger, with nothing but the thwarts above them—for the cabin was usually locked; or choose out some hollow of the links where the wind might whistle overhead. There the coats would be unbuttoned and the bull's-eyes discovered; and in the chequering glimmer, under the huge windy hall of the night, and cheered by a rich steam of toasting tinware, these fortunate young gentlemen would crouch together in the cold sand of the links or on the scaly bilges of the fishing boat."

One of these early companions, signing himself Lantern-Bearer, has provided us with a vivid picture of how he first met R.L.S. on the seashore:

"The Black Rock was an Alp to be climbed, and I had, with another playfellow, a dear cousin now long dead, begun the ascent. The rock was very hot and dry, and polished in places by the many feet that had gripped in its few nitches. Just at the top I found I had the wrong foot foremost, nothing to hold on to, and a sensation of fear. My head barely reached the top, but my hat did. To my relief, a thin brown hand with long fingers came over the edge of the rock, and a thin brown face, with very keen interested gray-brown eyes, looked over. 'Take my hand' said a boy's voice, and the fingers curved for the grip. I looked at the very thin, very long wrist that reached out of a pepper-and-salt shabby coat, and hesitated to trust to it, it looked very unequal to any efficient help, then up to the eager gray eyes bent on me, and felt that I might trust to the owner's willingness. 'All right,' I said, and put a sandy paw in the thin one. 'Hold tight and change your foot'; then, 'One, two, three,' and a good pull landed me on the top. 'I am Louis Stevenson?' the boy said. 'I was lying up here in the sun, on the warm rock. Isn't it fine?' "

They had a wonderful time together, these boys at North Berwick. There was a mound rising at the end of East Bay, and Louis thought that if they dug into it they might find the bones of dead Vikings. When the tide was out, they fished for large-headed, stout little fish called 'podleys':

"Here the falling tide leaves clear pools, in which shrimps dart and burrow. One day Louis and I were wading there, he with very skinny legs well displayed by much rolled-up thin trousers. 'Were you ever marooned?' he said suddenly, with the strange look in his eyes that always indicated with him 'an idea'. I was not at all sure what 'marooned' meant, but, unwilling to show my ignorance, said, 'No!' while wondering if it was something Louis meant to do to me. 'Well, look here, suppose you were on a desert island with nothing to eat, what would you do?' I had not the faintest idea, but suggested, 'Fish'. 'Silly, how could you catch fish in the sea? They aren't trout that one can guddle. Shrimps now— there are lots in the sand, and not bad to catch.'

I suggested that we should need a pot to boil them, remembering the pink dainties of a seaside tea-table.

'No,' said Louis, with sparkling eyes; 'raw would do. Father eats oysters, and I once had one; it wasn't very nice, but I heard him say they were very nourishing.'

'Oh Louis!' I cried. 'Those nasty gray things!'

'Yes,' he replied; 'I think shrimps much nicer-looking. Let us be marooned and try some.'

So we imagined ourselves alone in the wide ocean without food or fire. That was easy. Then we caught a few silver-brown wrigglers and paused.

'Where are we to begin, Louis?'

He looked at the morsel, and said slowly, 'The head would be best; it would die at once—bit quick!'

So we bit quick with sharp young teeth, and found the shrimp quite as good as Louis's oysters, but somehow the movement of the small fish made the meal more cannibalitis than the lethargic oyster would have done. It was, however, an experience added to our store, and Louis was always on the look-out for something new and uncommon . . . in his element anywhere that was off the beaten track, with possibilities of danger, otherwise adventure. His eyes glowed; his very hair, long and dank, seemed to stiffen into more elf-like locks. He always led the band, was always the master-spirit and inspiring force. A kind of magnetism seemed to emanate from him. . . . "

Occasionally grown-ups were allowed in on the magic of these holidays; an old gentleman called Mr. Girle used to hide a china egg while the girls and boys gathered around were under a vow to look the other way; whoever found it, scraping in the dry golden sand like rabbits or dogs, got sixpence from him. 'Lantern-Bearer' recalls feeling the bright glow of a fire at the core of almost all Louis Stevenson's invented games; and indeed, in the wind-swept cottage where they sometimes played, lighting and tending the fire was his share of the housekeeping. Nevertheless, one touch of envy appears in these affectionate recollections, for *he* was only allowed a wooden spade, and Louis an iron one, and this iron spade somehow put the latter on a pinnacle; we all know how much more sharply and cleanly they will cut into the smooth sand.

During a summer spent at Peebles, not with the Manse children but with a family of older cousins on the Stevenson side, he actually once fought a duel on the sands with real pistols and real powder; had they been real bullets too, he might never have lived to write of the wonderful duel between the brothers in *The Master of Ballantrae*; a chapter many would choose as the finest description of a duel ever written.

It is strange but true that any one who had half a chance of remembering Robert Louis Stevenson at any age, seemed quite unable to stop; there are books and books and more books full of these 'I remembers'. . . . And equally, while he was around, no boy seemed interested in ordinary games; he was always too full of suggestions for something altogether new and, if he could get away with it, dangerous; it was he who inspired them with the idea of making a kite of record size, and the first time it flew, it lifted one of them off his feet and carried him about fifty yards. Another time he started an ocean race with model yachts over a pretty stiff course from the harbour to a line about a mile out to sea. One might suppose that there was no such thing as school or education in his calendar; anyhow his education was always being interrupted by illness and travels abroad with his mother to recover from illness, his or hers. His father was unusual enough not to keep on worrying about the importance of school compared with the importance of his only son's health; most luckily for Smoutie, Thomas Stevenson had been an idler in his very early youth and always said that he learnt much more when away than by sitting screwed to his lessons. Education in the 1860's was very likely a much grimmer affair than it has since become; otherwise one could hardly believe that this highly respected citizen of Edinburgh, this industrious civil engineer, would, according to a reliable account, stop schoolboys in the street, look at their burden of books, shake his head over such trash, and advise them with earnestness to pay no heed to the rubbish which was being crammed into them. He begged them to look about them, play to their heart's content, but to read or study only what their inclination dictated. Never was Louis asked by his father how he stood in his classes. Not that he was let off teasing from this parent whom he adored and admired beyond all other people; one of his masters had remarked of him one day that his voice was "not strong, but impressive." Pleased with the praise, Louis carried it home and was ragged about it for years afterwards; whenever he raised his tone to a shrill excited pitch, Mr. Stevenson would listen gravely and then turn to a visitor and remark: "Louis is noted at school for his impressive voice"—till the boy would fly raging to his mother or his nurse to be soothed and petted; though no amount of spoiling from them was as sweet to him as one word of approval from that grave splendid father of his.

When barely seven, he was sent for a couple of hours every morning to Mr. Henderson's preparatory school not far from Heriot Row where

they lived; that was a success, for he considered
Mr. Henderson 'the most nicest man that ever
was'; but a severe attack of fever stopped it
after a few weeks; and it was two years later
before he was able to return to the same school.
When he was eleven, he went to the Edinburgh
Academy where several of his Balfour cousins were
already pupils. Here, being delicate and highly-
strung, he got mercilessly ragged, and fought back
like mad, but was glad when his father's lax
ideas allowed him to leave after a year and travel
to England and further abroad, to Germany and
the south of France and Italy. He was constantly
being taken away from Edinburgh, either for the
sake of his parents' health or his own, to visit
places in Scotland with lovely provocative names
—Dunoon, Lasswade, Bridge of Allan, Rothesay.
Once he was left at a school in London while his
parents were at Mentone, and wrote a letter in
French and English which he hoped would so
touch their hearts that they would allow him to
leave and join them. We wonder which was the
most effective in appealing to them, the awful
French that might easily have made them
consider he had better be brought along to
where it might improve, or the simple pathetic

appeal at the end which proved how unhappy he was?

Ma chere Maman,—Jai recu votre lettre Aujourdhui et comme le jour prochaine est mon jour de naisance je vous écrit ce lettre. Ma grande gatteaux est arrivé il leve 12 livres et demi le prix etait 17 shillings. Sur la soirée de Monseigneur Faux il y etait quelques belles feux d'artifice. Mais les polissons entrent dans notre champ et nos feux d'artifice et handkerchiefs disappeared quickly, but we charged them out of the field. Je suis presque driven mad par une bruit terrible tous les garcons kik up comme grand un bruit qu'il est possible. I hope you will find your house at Mentone nice. I have been obliged to stop from writing by the want of a pen, but now I have one, so I will continue.

My dear papa, you told me to tell you whenever I was miserable. I do not feel well, and I wish to get home. Do take me with you.

R. Stevenson.

At Mentone private tutors were provided for him in an irregular sort of attempt to keep up with his education and not let it be forgotten altogether till he was old enough to go to Edinburgh University.

It was from a previous short bout of school in Torquay (when he was about sixteen) that he wrote home to his father for funds; a gay, impudent epistle; its anticlimax, setting the minimum sum at two shillings and sixpence, shows that Thomas Stevenson's son and heir was certainly not overloaded with pocket money:

Respected Paternal Relative,—I write to make a request of the most moderate nature. Every year I have cost you an enormous—nay, elephantine— sum of money for drugs and physician's fees, and the most expensive time of the twelve months was March.

But this year the biting Oriental blasts, the howling tempests, and the general ailments of the human race have been successfully braved by yours truly.

Does not this deserve remuneration?

I appeal to your charity, I appeal to your generosity, I appeal to your justice, I appeal to your accounts, I appeal, in fine, to your purse.

My sense of generosity forbids the receipt of more—my sense of justice forbids the receipt of less—than half-a-crown.—Greeting from, Sir, your most affectionate and needy son,

R. Stevenson.

On the whole and considering he was an only child, he was allowed a good time as a boy without too much pampering. He had a pony and became a reckless rider; his cousins Bob and Katherine also had ponies which he named Hell and Heaven; for his own was Purgatory. They used to ford the Tweed, galloping right through from Peebles to Innerleithan, and race along the Queen's highway with the thin brown boy who led them shouting: "Hell wins, I say; don't hold Heaven in, you stupid. No; I believe Purgatory will beat you both." Or sometimes for a change they were moss-troopers out a-rieving or flying full-speed past every ambush of the English to the shelter of their own peel tower. The two boys also enjoyed galloping through the toll bars, pretending to run a blockade; but the girl, being more law-abiding, would pay the tax and soothe the angry toll-keeper.

If Louis happened to like a subject, he took a glowing interest in it and gathered quantities of extraordinary information from all sorts of odd sources; his foreign languages were naturally good, for he had had the advantage of hearing French, German and Italian spoken in France, Germany and Italy; but he was as wild and inattentive as might have been expected on subjects that were outside literature and history; as for his spelling, it was not only pretty funny for his age, but remained so till the day of his death.

Not a settled life? No, nor ever would be; 'settled' was a word that need not have existed for Robert Louis Stevenson.

CHAPTER THREE

ALL the same, he very nearly did have a settled address when he was seventeen. Had it not been for his health, that persistent bogey forever chasing him into foreign countries, who can tell but that Swanston Cottage, snugly set in a fold of the Pentland Hills, would have been his address for the rest of his life. You can read about Swanston if you want to, in *St. Ives*; the Chevalier St. Ives is hidden there by Flora and Ronald after his daring escape down the sheer walls of Edinburgh Castle.

In 1867, Thomas Stevenson took this stone cottage at the foot of the meadows sloping up to Allermuir, Caerketton and Halkerside, to live in with his family every year from March to October; he had begun to dread those long winters when his wife and son had to go away to the south of France because they were not strong enough to stand a northern climate, leaving him alone and disconsolate for weeks to go to and fro between his offices in George Street and a silent, solitary house in Heriot Row.

Although Swanston is only half an hour from Edinburgh, nobody would imagine it was not in the very heart of the country. The village, no more than a cluster of cottages, would have been out of sight from their old-fashioned garden; sheep wandered beyond, freely nibbling at the grass, and the burn rippled and sang within sight and sound of their windows. There was an old tree at Swanston Cottage where R.L.S. light-heartedly carved his own and his family's initials when they first came; it is never really a particularly good idea to cut one's initials on trees nor on anything else, but in this special case one cannot help feeling a little sorry that the tree has blown down, so that one has no chance of visualising the tall lean youth of seventeen, with Coolin (the terrier given him on his seventh birthday) standing by and watching his master cutting deep in the bark those famous initials which the author of *Peter Pan* once said were the most beloved in the literature of their land.

When Coolin died, R.L.S. wrote his epitaph to be inscribed in Latin on a wooden panel:

38

Photo J. Allan Cash

"The Hills of Home"—The Pentland Hills above Swanston

"To Coolin, the gentle and friendly, who in a green old age, by some unhappy chance, met with his death at the place where three roads meet, where the hunters are wont to gather. This stone has been set up to his memory by his sorrowing friends. 1869. R.L.S."

But while Coolin was still alive, he wrote of him:

"Coolin was a thief to the last; among a thousand peccadilloes, a whole goose and a whole leg of mutton lay upon his conscience."

From the first, Louis loved Swanston and felt at home and happy there, away from the smoke of Auld Reekie (a pet name which the citizens of Edinburgh affectionately gave their home town); he loved it especially when he was in exile and knew all his doctors had forbidden him ever to go back. He was a tremendous walker, and grew to know all those hills and their bloodstained history, battlefields of the Romans and the Picts; centuries later, it was the scene of the 'forty-five Rebellion; and then the Covenanters encamped there before they fell at Rullion Green:

Grey recumbent tombs of the dead in desert
    places,
Standing stones on the vacant wine-red moor,
Hills of sheep, and the homes of the silent
    vanquished races,
And winds, austere and pure;

He made friends with all the local characters,
shepherds and farm hands; on one of his walks,
possibly at the foot of Caerketton with its seven
long white scars running down the hillside like
waterfalls, he was startled by a wrathful shout:
"C'way oot among the sheep!" That was John
Todd, known as the Roaring Shepherd. Presently
the pair learnt to hit it off beautifully, and both
John and the old Scottish gardener at Swanston
went into the rich and varied pageant of Steven-
son's odd friends, which were to include King
Tembinoka of Apemama; King Kalakua of
Honolulu; Ori a Ori, a warrior chief; Mataafa,
defeated King of Samoa; Professor Fleeming
Jenkin, scholar and professor of Edinburgh
University; W. E. Henley, poet and editor;
Sydney Colvin, Curator of the British Museum;
Henry James, the American author; Charles
Baxter, Writer to the Signet of Edinburgh; various

missionaries of all denominations; Valentine Roche, their French 'bonne' who followed him from Hyères to Bournemouth, thence to the Adirondacks and San Francisco, and on his first voyage to the South Seas; Sosimo, his personal servant at Samoa, and the Bakers who looked after him at Saranac and forgave him when he burnt holes in their sheets with his cigarettes; naval officers from H.M.S. *Curaçoa*; Will Low, the American artist; and Count Nerli who painted him looking like the most rakish of his own pirates (neither his mother nor his wife liked that portrait, but Stevenson declared it was more like him than any other!); St. Gaudens, the sculptor whose medallion of R.L.S. can be seen on the wall of St. Giles in Edinburgh; Jean Simoneau, the inkeeper at Monterey who nursed him when he was near death; every doctor who ever attended him; Adelaide Boodle, a young girl in Bournemouth who was always in and out of the house. And Lloyd Osbourne—well, he can hardly be counted, as he was a sort of near relation. . . .

Yes, he was good at making friends; good at keeping them.

In the years after they took Swanston Cottage,

several things, nice and horrid, happened to
Louis Stevenson; mostly horrid. His idling days
were supposed to be over, so he was enrolled at
Edinburgh University for the study of Latin and
Greek. When he came back after the first long
Summer Vacation he gave up Greek, and became
friends with Professor Fleeming Jenkin who had
been appointed to the Chair of Engineering.
Fleeming Jenkin was to be more than just a
University friend; Louis was always happy at
their house, talking and arguing, working off
steam, and sometimes acting in their plays, for
Mrs. Jenkin was a gifted amateur actress. Once,
after a performance of Sophocles' tragedies, two
of the young actors did an improvised war-dance
when the final curtain came down, and then threw
themselves at opposite ends of a couch, their
feet lifted and meeting in a triumphal arch in
the middle. . . . Louis, in the wings, took a look
at the tableau, touched a spring—and up went
the curtain again. Naturally the audience roared
with laughter; Professor Jenkin, who had been
watching this part of the play from the front, went
behind the scenes: "Mr. Stevenson," he said
grimly, "I shall ask you to give me a few minutes
in my own room." R.L.S. always said ruefully

that those were among the worst few minutes of his life!

Nevertheless, if by sternness or persuasion, anyone could have influenced this young loafer to do some honest work, Fleeming Jenkin would have been the man; for Louis not only liked but respected him, perhaps because he found quite early in their relationship as pupil and master that he could not wangle out of him a certificate of attendance at his classes after a whole session of non-attendance, as he had disgracefully succeeded in doing with the absent-minded Professor Blackie. But in the case of Professor Jenkin, the reply was a decided: "No, Mr. Stevenson. There may be doubtful cases; there is no doubt about yours. You have simply *not* attended my classes." We have Stevenson's own word for this, because when he was a famous author, and Fleeming Jenkin died, R.L.S. wrote his life, trying conscientiously and with touching diligence to make it a worth-while tribute to his friend, perhaps with the idea of atoning for past truancies.

He says himself he was an idle unpopular student; and but for the sanctuary of the Jenkins' home always ready to welcome him when he was in hot water everywhere else, heaven knows what would have become of him. It is no use pretending that his University career was satisfactory, judged by the usual standards. He did not spend his time, he squandered it; but we should remember that this was as much his father's fault as his own, for teaching him to think so lightly, in the past, of the value of regular education. And life at a Scottish University was so very different from life at Oxford and Cambridge, where English lads were cut off from ordinary experience and liberty, to live in a world of gardens—

". . . At an earlier age the Scottish lad begins the greatly different experience of crowded classrooms, of a gaunt quadrangle, of a bell hourly booming over the traffic of the city to recall him from the streets where he had been wandering fancy-free. . . . Our tasks ended, we of the North go forth as freemen into the humming, lamplit city . . . no proctor lies in wait to intercept us; till the bell sounds again we are masters of the world."

If we do not give ourselves permission at this point to look ahead, we may be in danger of summing up Robert Louis Stevenson as being in truth what the sober respectable burghers of Edinburgh thought of him: an incurable impenitent loafer without a conscience. Yet once he was at his own job of writing, and others dependent on his efforts, he refused to allow illness to get him down, but went on slogging ceaselessly and never let himself be satisfied with work carelessly done, either.

Yet it was odd that all the high spirits and gaiety and generosity with which he was presently to charm the world, did not, at this stage, succeed in charming his fellow-students; most of them had to buckle down to it seriously for the sake of the future, and may have thought it unfair that young Stevenson, with a rich father, should have idled quite so defiantly. One of them described him, with a disapproving frown, as taking very little part in the work of the classes he *did* attend:

"He used to sit on a far-back bench, pencil in hand, and with a notebook before him, and looking as if he were taking notes of the lectures. But in reality he took no notes, and seldom listened to the lectures. 'I prefer,' he used to say, 'to spend the time in writing original nonsense of my own.' He always carried in his pocket a note-book, which he sometimes called his 'Book of Original Nonsense', and not only during the class hour, but at all odd times, he jotted down thoughts and fancies in prose and verse."

Thomas Stevenson was not quite as foolishly indulgent as he seemed; he had his own dreams for Louis, and they were connected with bringing him into the family firm of Engineers to the Commissioners of Northern Lights. His pride in the splendid inheritance, in the Lighthouse Stevensons, survived those first dawdling months at the University; he was only impatient to see his son begin on the practical side of engineering; and during the first Long Vacation he had sent Louis to Anstruther on the coast of Fife, to watch some harbour construction going on there. And now we see how that far-off trouble lying in wait all these years between father and son who loved each other so tenderly, is willy-nilly drawing nearer; soon, not quite yet, but soon, Thomas would have to learn that inheritance or not, Louis was no engineer. Already he wrote home quite frankly: how awful, he said, that he should draw so slowly and so badly, constantly forgetting to take measurements; and in an utterly homesick letter written in confidence to his mother, he confessed he was sick of 'this grey, grim, sea-beaten hole,' and longing to get back among trees and flowers:

"Write by return of post, and tell me what to do. If possible, I should like to cut the business and come right slick out to Swanston."

He was not allowed to come 'right slick out' to Swanston, but sent up to Wick, on the stormy north-east coast not far from the Orkney Islands. Here, strangely enough, he appeared less unhappy than when he was nearer home; perhaps the grandeur of the wild rocky scenery with its cliffs and caves and the big seas, thrilled him; or perhaps he happened to like the people better than those at Anstruther. He really did rough it there, going out at night in the lighter, and doing stern jobs that skinned and blistered his hands, hauling on ropes and the anchor line to get in the great wet hawser that soaked them all to the skin . . . discovering that to coil a stiff wet rope in the dark in drenching rain and mist and grey squalls, beset by high waves and foam and spray,

47

was not quite the same as playing at boats with his little cousins on the stairs at the Manse. But he had no right to have bribed a scamp of a diver to let him go down under water in a diver's outfit:

"It was grey, harsh, easterly weather, the swell ran pretty high . . . when I found myself at last on the diver's platform, twenty pounds of lead upon each foot and my whole person swollen with ply and ply of woollen underclothing. One moment, the salt wind was whistling round my night-capped head; the next, I was crushed almost double under the weight of the helmet. As that intolerable burthen was laid upon me, I could have found it in my heart (only for shame's sake) to cry off from the whole enterprise. But it was too late. The attendants began to turn the hurdy-gurdy, and the air to whistle through the tube; some one screwed in the barred window of the vizor; and I was cut off in a moment from my fellow-men; standing there in their midst, but quite divorced from intercourse; a creature deaf and dumb, pathetically looking forth upon them from a climate of his own. Except that I could move and feel, I was like a man fallen in a

48

catalepsy. But time was scarce given me to realise my isolation; the weights were hung upon my back and breast, the signal-rope was thrust into my unresisting hand; and setting a twenty-pound foot upon the ladder, I began ponderously to descend."

The harbour at Wick had to be abandoned, and Louis returned for his second winter at the University. In the summer of 1870 he went with Fleeming Jenkins' Engineering Classes on various expeditions; one to the little island of Earraid, off Mull, where the deep-sea lighthouse of Dun Heartach was being built—(and where Louis conveniently arranged to have David Balfour shipwrecked, in *Kidnapped*). Then on to Skye in the Hebrides, entering the loch at midnight by the light of flickering torches; and that, too, was very much to his taste. Long afterwards he wrote his own sad words to the haunting lilt of the Skye Boat Song, wishing he were young again and back on the steamer *Clansman*:

> Sing me a song of a lad that is gone,
>   Say, could that lad be I?
> Merry of soul he sailed on a day
>   Over the sea to Skye.

Mull was astern, Rum on the port,
    Eigg on the starboard bow;
Glory of youth glowed in his soul;
    Where is that glory now?

This tour began a more congenial period of
companionship and stimulation; Louis was admitted to a well-known Society in Edinburgh
known as the Spec, with a great library and a hall
for its debates; he felt himself highly honoured
by his inclusion, not aware that one day his own
name would be quoted after Sir Walter Scott's, as
its second most famous member.

Have you ever played a sort of comparing
game with yourself called little-did-I-think? All
sorts of queer surprising contrasts are likely to
come up. And certainly this boy of nineteen who
gazed with awe at the faces lit by the glowing red
fire and the soft light of wax candles, on the night
when in a tense state of nerves he made his first
speech to the Spec, could have had no idea that
in the far distant future, years later, other
students, no doubt equally strained and nervous
and intent on doing well, would see hung on the
wall directly opposite them, down the room and
over the fireplace—

50

What would they see?

A flag; the ensign of the *Casco*, the yacht in which Robert Louis Stevenson was to make his first voyage to the South Pacific; it covered his bier when native chiefs carried him up the steep track of the mountain to his last resting-place in Samoa.

Thomas Stevenson must have been growing more and more anxious during these University years, as Louis grew daily more reckless and wayward. He was actually run in by the police during a Town and Gown snowball fight, and bound over to keep the peace, and that could hardly have been much fun for the well-placed highly respected Stevensons. In March 1871, unusually youthful for such an honour, he won a medal and read a paper at the Royal Society of Arts, on his father's invention—"A New Form of Intermittent Light for Lighthouses"—but that moment of glory could hardly have provided more than a flicker of hope that perhaps now all would be well.

It might have been a mistake on the part of his parents to think they could keep him out of mischief by giving him only an absurdly small amount of pocket money, £1 a month; hardly

likely that anyone with young Stevenson's nature
would allow it to interfere with his extravagance
and hot-headed rebellious determination to have
his own way; he would find a way to get money
somehow. One day Mrs. Stevenson was driving
with her sister Jane and another relation along
the High Street, and telling 'Auntie' some of their
troubles with Lou, when the other relation interrupted them with: *"Do* look at that queer old-
bones-man!" Auntie glanced at the ragamuffin
slouching along the pavement with a huge bag of
bones over his shoulder: "Oh, Louis, Louis, what
will you do next?"

What Louis Stevenson did next was to confess
to his father, on one of their long walks from
Swanston, that he desired to give up engineering,
give up any question of entering the firm, for he
wanted instead to become a writer and devote his
whole life to that profession. It can hardly have
been a pleasant walk for either of them; although
he had been encouraged to write ever since he was
five. Yet Thomas Stevenson was very decent
about it; there was no thunder and lightning, as
on that dreadful walk a year later when he was to
discover that Louis was going through a phase of
pretending to care nothing for religion. All the

ame, he was not going to give in altogether; he suggested a compromise: his son could give up engineering, but he would have to have a safe and regular profession, and it was no good arguing that authorship could ever be that; he had better train for the Bar. So Louis agreed to take Law classes at the University.

Three years later he was a full-blown barrister. His cousin Etta has recorded the scene of delirious excitement and joy when they drove into town in the big open barouche to hear the examination results . . . and Lou insisted on sitting on top of the carriage with his feet on the seat between his father and mother, and kept on waving his hat and calling out like mad to the passers-by that he had passed his examination for the Bar. That was all very fine, but the exact sum of four guineas was all he ever earned by practising Law; for he had fixed it up with his mother that he was always to keep the pounds and she get the shillings on his briefs, and she remembered receiving four shillings and no more from that source. Now that he had achieved what his father had asked of him, he declared his intention of retiring from the Law to dedicate himself wholly and entirely to writing. Poor Thomas Stevenson had not only to face this disappointment of all his hopes, but could not forget the terrible quarrels they had been having all that winter; he was upset by hearing lurid rumours of the young man's follies, and disapproved intensely of his companions and way of life; he would gladly have died for his son, but thought that to keep him at home and entirely dependent, would work out 'for his own good' in the end. It worked out that their relationship went from bad to worse; there were constant scenes and quarrels . . . and then a crisis. Louis' father was not the stodgy type of heavy parent; he also had nerves and imagination. Louis could not be careless of the unhappiness he was causing; he could not give in either, but made himself really ill. Perhaps to ease the situation, they sent him to stay with some English cousins at a Rectory in Suffolk. This turned out to be a very lucky decision, for there he met Mrs. Sitwell who took an interest in his writing and in turn introduced him to her special friend whom she was to marry a great many years later, Sidney Colvin, a Fellow of Trinity College, Cambridge. These two for the next few years had more influence than anyone else who had hitherto come into Stevenson's life; they were convinced

54

he was a born writer, encouraged him and gave him the confidence in himself which he sorely needed, and were responsible for his first few essays written and published. They also made him go to London to consult a famous physician about his health; Sir Andrew Clark found him suffering from nervous exhaustion and a threat of lung trouble, and ordered him south to the Riviera.

That winter of lounging in the sunshine, and alone, did a lot for him; when he went back to Edinburgh, he was in a much happier state of mind. He had begun to have his essays accepted and to earn money, and at least had a right to call himself an author—only spending about five times as much as he ever earned; though usually on others, not on himself.

Having no brothers or sisters, friends meant an enormous lot to him. Professor Fleeming Jenkin, Mrs. Sitwell and Sidney Colvin had headed the list hitherto; but two years afterwards came that striking encounter, in Edinburgh Infirmary, with the English poet Henley who was to be his greatest friend of all until a tragic quarrel which after thirteen years was to smash between them and separate them for ever.

Meanwhile, let's have a look at their first

meeting. The editor of a magazine which had published some stuff by both these promising newcomers, happened to be visiting Edinburgh, and took Louis along with him to the Infirmary to see a big hearty yellow-bearded giant in bed, desperately poor and still almost unknown; Henley had lost one foot from tuberculosis and come up to Edinburgh in the hope that the other could be saved by the famous surgeon Lister. In bed in the same room with Henley were two little boys of seven and six, Roden and Willie, cheerful little fellows who used to play at operations. . . . They must have had a sudden wonderful surprise listening to the talk between two grown-up men; but not the usual sort of boring grown-up talk; actually—listen, Roden and Willie!—they were talking about *pirates*!

Henley was eighteen months shut up in that hospital ward, but at last he was able to go out for a drive; and Louis somehow managed to carry him down the stairs to the carriage; it was worth it, he declared enthusiastically, to see the splendour shine from Henley's eyes at being brought again in touch with the outside world:

"It is now just the top of spring with us. The

whole country is mad with green. To see the cherry-blossom bitten out upon the black firs, and the black firs bitten out of the blue sky, was a sight to set before a king."

Always restless for any new and active experience that came his way, R.L.S. was doing a lot more than writing essays and talking to Henley in the Infirmary; walking-tours and skating came into his programme; and he was an expert at canoeing. A little boy of about twelve, George Lisle, remembers how he and five other lads were staying for the holidays on the Island of Cramond in the Firth of Forth, and saw through their telescope two canoes struggling up from Granton in the teeth of a high wind, the sea washing perilously over their cockleshell craft. Somehow they got into calm water; and the boys rushed down to welcome the mariners:

"The first to land was a lanky, cadaverous, black-haired, black-eyed man, apparently six feet in height but very slim, in a velveteen coat. . . . As I was the biggest of the lot of wreckers who had come to welcome them, the canoeists asked me if I would help them up with their canoes above high-water mark, as they had had enough sailing for

57   E

one day and were badly in need of a rest. I was delighted at the job, and as I was accustomed to climb among the rocks and over slippery sea-weed, and did not mind getting myself wet, it was not long before the two canoes were safely above high-water mark. He of the canvas canoe immediately lay down to rest in the sunshine, but the other before doing so thanked me in the nicest possible way for my stalwart assistance, and presented me with a shilling. . . . Among other questions he asked of the half-dozen of us, who were all about the age of twelve—

'What other savages live upon the island?'

I felt somewhat nettled at being called a savage, and replied: 'You must have forgotten your *Robinson Crusoe* or you would know that it was the savages who came to the island in canoes. There were no savages till you came.'

Both the voyagers laughed heartily, and he of the canvas canoe said to the other: 'You're fairly caught this time, Louis.' "

After that, Stevenson often used to take young George canoeing; once to Inchmickery Island in one of the deepest channels in the Firth of Forth:

"We explored the whole place and paddled right round it and the adjacent Oxcar Rock and the Cow and Calves Islands, which were shining in all their beauty, and returned pretty well tired, but thoroughly pleased with our adventure."

Louis must have had an unquenchable taste for canoeing, and indeed for any chance to travel that came his way, always longing to get to the back of beyond. He went off to live for a time with his cousin Bob and a whole colony of young artists in the Forest of Fontainebleau; English, American, French, Scandanavian; they and their friend Sir Walter Simpson were the only Scots. Walter Simpson had been a student at Edinburgh University with Louis; he was the son of Sir James Simpson who gave chloroform to the world; a quiet, cautious, slow, kind young man; when he and Louis went off on an inland voyage in canoes through the rivers and waterways of Belgium and Northern France, starting from the Antwerp docks, it was the *Arethusa* (Louis) who was always in trouble—once he was nearly arrested—and the *Cigarette* (Walter) who got him out of it. You can read about their innumerable adventures in the first book Stevenson ever wrote: *An Inland*

Voyage. The French peasantry and innkeepers were puzzled by this odd pair, their behaviour and Louis' terrible clothes, and usually ended by supposing them to be pedlars; if it were a prosperous inn, then the pedlars had bad treatment, sent round to the back door or driven away altogether; when it was a more humble *auberge,* then peddling was in itself a rich and prosperous occupation, and they were honoured, given the best table and the best food.

When Louis got back, a short time after Simpson, to the little riverside village of Grez, on the edge of the Forest, he moored his canoe on the shores of the Loing, crossed the garden at dusk on a September evening and looked through the open window to the lamp-lit dining-room where his artist friends were all gathered round the table; for the first time, the colony of men had been invaded by two women, or rather a woman and a girl; he had heard a rumour beforehand of the arrival of Fanny Osbourne with her young daughter Belle and her little son Lloyd, and had prophesied darkly that their presence would be the beginning of the end, quite sure that the ladies must spoil everything. Little Lloyd Osbourne, aged eight, had been equally in dread of the re-arrival at the Inn of those 'terrible Stevensons', afraid that they would force them to leave.

The older of the two ladies, dark and grave and beautiful, turned and saw him standing at the window . . . Their eyes met . . . Then he vaulted in, his knapsack on his back, and all the artists, about eighteen of them, cheered at the sight of their popular high-spirited comrade.

From that moment and for the rest of his life, nothing was ever to be the same again for Louis; he had fallen headlong in love.

CHAPTER FOUR

FANNY OSBOURNE had been brought up in the backwoods of Indianapolis, a free tomboy childhood. Like Louis, she was a born rebel, with courage and strength of mind that could battle through all adversities that came along, including six awful years in a cabin in a rough mining camp in Nevada, where her first husband, a gambler by nature, was trying his luck at the silver mines. A strange wife for the son of a highly respected Edinburgh engineer to have chosen.

They could not be married yet, because Sam Osbourne was still alive in San Francisco. All the same, that was a wonderful summer at Grez. Belle, who was sixteen, and Lloyd, who was eight, never forgot the zest and joyousness which their new playmate brought into all their days; they had games on the river, they bathed, they raced in canoes that capsized, Belle said, if you as much as winked; but they were all so happy, nobody seemed to care much if they were wet or dry, in the river or out of it. Fanny could not swim a stroke, and when her canoe upset, clung to it till someone rescued her. Their simple food, perfectly cooked, sounds like a perpetual picnic:

"Yard-long loaves of bread, cheese made in the village, lettuce salad flavoured with garlic and tarragon, chickens roasted on a spit before the open fire, all accompanied by bottles of good red wine."

On rainy evenings they played charades or made up verses or drew cartoons all over the walls. For two more summers the little company went on meeting at Grez. And while Louis and Fanny went off with their easels and satchels and painting materials into the forest, Lloyd used to sit for hours on the bridge with his pole and line, hoping for the best. 'Petit feesh' was his nickname among the village boys at Grez, because the peasants used to pass him with a pleasant 'Bonjour', and not understanding, thinking they enquired what he was doing there, he always answered with "Fish".

During the winter, while the Osbournes stayed in Paris, Louis did not return often to Scotland;

London, Paris and Grez were his haunts. He wrote some fine exciting short stories and was beginning to make his name. So far, he had only published one complete book, but in the autumn of 1878 he had the idea of going off alone on a twelve-days' tramp through the mountains of the Cevennes, afterwards to write a book about what befell him. 'Alone' is the wrong word, however; he took with him a sturdy little grey donkey, Modestine, not to ride but to carry his fleecy blue sleeping-bag on her back and various other packs and baggages. Through *Travels With a Donkey in the Cevennes*, Modestine became almost as famous as her master, and as popular, which she certainly did not deserve, for she was a wayward obstinate little brute, full of unexpected tricks; perhaps the only living creature who did not at once respond to Louis' charm. But even in a recent competition set for juveniles, when the children had to write an essay on 'Your favourite character in Stevenson', Modestine came out second in the list, between Long John Silver who was first, and Alan Breck, the daring boastful Highlander from *Kidnapped*, third.

Meanwhile, Fanny thought it her duty to take Belle and Lloyd back to their home in California.

Louis did not imagine he would ever see her again. As for young Lloyd, he was broken-hearted at the parting; he in his turn might have done a little-did-I-think on the theme of those future years with his friend and hero who was also to become his step-father and collaborator: little did he think that in three years time they were to share every home together, in Scotland, Switzerland, the south of France, Bournemouth, and high up in Adirondack Mountains; that he was to have a book written entirely to please him and dedicated to him: *Treasure Island*, one of the most famous books in the world; that together they were to sail the South Seas from one group of tropical islands to another, face the same dangers, and finally settle down in a house they were to build half-way up Mount Vaea in Samoa. No, when they parted, Lloyd, aged ten, could not have consoled himself with any glimpse of these exciting happenings.

Louis stayed in London with Henley during most of 1878, and wrote stories that were published in a magazine called *London* of which Henley had just become editor. The very title of the series: 'The New Arabian Nights', starts us off expecting something very strange and fantastic, like the sort of incidents that happened in Baghdad long ago, when the Sultan and the Grand Vizier walked disguised about the streets. Only these tales were set in London in Stevenson's own day; and the first was called *The Young Man With the Cream Tarts.* He and his painter cousin, Bob Stevenson, had a glorious time working them out, full of absurdities, perils and freakish encounters that were not quite impossible for any adventurous spirit and might be waiting just round the next corner. But oddly enough, at that period they were not a success, nor was the magazine itself, though Henley and Stevenson enjoyed being journalists, editor and chief contributor, always in a hurry and for ever discussing what their next success was to be. Louis may have had some sort of idea that he was only marking time and waiting for a summons from the other end of the world; but Henley, who was like a roaring lion going for a walk with a brilliant graceful antelope by his side, was bewildered and bitterly disappointed, a disappointment from which he was never to recover, when suddenly Stevenson threw up everything, broke his career, deserted his friends, and went off with no money and in a rotten state of health,

66

because Fanny had sent him a letter from California to say she was ill and could bear their separation no longer. Louis dared not tell his parents beforehand, he knew how it would hurt them; already he had had a hard job to stand up against Henley and all his other friends' robust attempts at dissuasion. He wrote to his father from on board the s.s. *Devonia*, for he would accept no help nor money for this wild errand on an emigrant ship, feeling it had to be done off his own bat. It was high time, he told himself, that he took real risks, and found out the meaning of real hardship.

Crossing the Atlantic was then a slow crowded comfortless affair; you must read his book about it, *The Amateur Emigrant*, to get some idea of the noise, the bad food, the smells; add to that his terrible loneliness, and we get some notion that the delicate only child of the rich Stevensons of Edinburgh came out pretty strong from this first severe test of courage. Yet he did not just bemoan his fate nor walk about the steerage deck looking noble and sad and aloof, but helped his fellow-passengers with their encumbrances of children, nursed them when they were sick, cheered them up, joked with them and even organised singsongs and other entertainments to break up the sodden misery of their tossing days and nights. From his point of view, the worst of the journey was still ahead; he was always and all his life better at sea than on land. The stampede in the Customs-shed on their arrival at New York reads like a minor revolution without any of its glory; and next came the horrible journey in an emigrant train across America from end to end, when he became more and more ill and still would not give in. The train took a fortnight; now, even if you do not fly, you can cross from the Atlantic to the Pacific in three and a half days. Yet one of the things we remember most clearly from his published journal of *Across the Plains* (because he remembered it so clearly himself) was how a news-boy—(perpetually walking up and down bawling out his wares: papers, fruit, lollipops, and cigars; soap, towels, tin washing-dishes, tin coffee pitchers, hash or beans and bacon)—noticing this bony feverish skeleton of a man propping open the door with his leg for the sake of getting some fresh air, suddenly came up behind him, touched his shoulder and put a large juicy pear into his hand, bought from his meagre earnings.

There is another game, the same kind as little-did-I-think, that one can play inside one's own head to cheer oneself up during a particularly bad time; and if Stevenson had never discovered it before (he probably had) it came to him while crossing America in the emigrant train: the game of it-might-have-been-much-worse. He was grateful to the train that carried them safely and swiftly through so many hidden perils, such as the ferocity of Indians, and in contrast quotes a letter written twenty years earlier by a boy of eleven who had done the same journey in a covered wagon:

My dear sister Mary—I am afraid you will go nearly crazy when you read my letter. If Jerry (the writer's eldest brother) has not written to you before now, you will be surprised to hear that we are in California, and that poor Thomas (another brother, of fifteen) is dead. We started from —— in July, with plenty of provisions and too yoke oxen. We went along very well till we got within six or seven hundred miles of California, when the Indians attacked us. We found places where they had killed the emigrants. We had one passenger with us, too guns, and one revolver; so we ran all the lead We had into bullets (and) hung the guns up in the wagon so that we could get at them in a minit. It was about two o'clock in the afternoon; droave the cattel a little way; when a prairie chicken alited a little way from the wagon.

Jerry took out one of the guns to shoot it, and told Tom to drive the oxen. Tom and I drove the oxen, and Jerry and the passenger went on. Then, after a little, I left Tom and caught up with Jerry and the other man. Jerry stopped for Tom to come up; me and the man went on and sit down by a little stream. In a few minutes, we heard some noise; then three shots (they all struck poor Tom, I suppose); then they gave the war hoop, and as many as twenty of the red skins came down upon us. The three that shot Tom was hid by the side of the road in the bushes.

I thought that Tom and Jerry were shot; so I told the other man that Tom and Jerry were dead, and that we had better try to escape, if possible. I had no shoes on; having a sore foot, I thought I would not put them on. The man and me run down the road, but We was soon stopt by an Indian on a pony. We then turend the other way, and run up the side of the Mountain, and hid behind some cedar trees, and stayed there till dark. The Indians hunted all over after us, and verry close to us, so close that we could here there omyhawks Jingle. At dark the man and me started on, I stubing my toes against sticks and stones. We traveld on all night; and next morning, Just as it was getting gray, we saw something n the shape of a man. It layed Down in the grass. We went up to it, and it was Jerry. He thought we were Indians. You can imagine how glad he was to see me. He thought we was all dead but him, and we thought him and Tom was dead. He had the gun that he took out of the wagon to shoot the prairie Chicken; all he had was the load that was in it.

We traveld on till about eight o'clock, We caught up with one wagon with too men in it. We had traveld with them before one day; we stopt and they Drove on; we knew that they was ahead of us, unless they had been killed too. My feet was so sore when we caught up with them that I Had to ride; I could not step. We traveld on for too days, when the men that owned the cattle said they could not drive them another inch. We unyoked the oxen; we had about seventy pounds of flour; we took it out and divided it into four packs. Each of the men took about 18 pounds apiece and

71

a blanket. I carried a little bacon, dried meat, and little quilt; I had in all about twelve pounds. We had one pint of flour a day for our alloyance. Sometimes we made soup of it; sometimes we (made) pancakes; and sometimes mixed it up with cold water and eat it that way. We traveld twelve or fourteen days. The time came at last when we should have to reach some place or starve. We saw fresh horse and cattle tracks. The morning come, we scraped all the flour out of the sack, mixed it up, and baked it into bread; and made some soup, and eat everything we had. We traveld on all day without anything to eat, and that evening we Caught up with a sheep train of eight wagons. We traveld with them till we arrived at the settlements; and now I am safe in California, and got to good home, and going to school.

Disaster did not end for Louis when at last they reached San Francisco. He found news from Fanny that she was better and had gone to Monterey, so he started to work his way towards her; and being by now penniless, took a job as a cowboy about twenty miles from Monterey; he was, of course, quite unfit for it, lost his way, fel

in a faint from his horse, and lay out under a tree
in a sort of stupor for three days and nights somewhere on an Angora goat-ranch in the Santa
Lucia Mountains. Here he was found and nursed
by an old frontiersman: 'a mighty hunter of
bears', till he was able to drag along to Monterey,
and there again collapsed on the doorstep of Jules
Simoneau, who kept a café. Jules Simoneau, like
the newsboy who gave him the pear, like the old
bear-hunter on the goat ranch, like all those odd
friends that R.L.S. was to pick up at all times
of his life whenever he was derelict, became
entirely devoted to his patient. He remarked a
long time afterwards to a Stevenson lover visiting
Monterey:

"Ah! 'Zat was Louis! Louis 'e was brave.
W'at you t'ink? 'E was ver' poor. 'E was ver'
seeck. Oui! sometam' 'e was ver' ongry. But
always 'e laugh. Always 'e keep ze smile! Always
'e try to work, even w'en it seem 'is heart break.
Zat was Louis. 'E was *brave*!"

Monterey was the ancient Mexican capital on
the Pacific; the great breakers, vast and green,
roll up the long beaches, sometimes bringing in

F

the bones of whales to scatter like treasure on the sand. Long afterwards, Stevenson wrote a poem to little Louis Sanchez, his godchild who still lived there:

Now that you have spelt your lesson, lay it down
    and go and play,
Seeking shells and seaweed on the sands of
    Monterey,
Watching all the mighty whalebones, lying buried
    by the breeze,
Tiny sandy-pipers, and the huge Pacific seas.

He recovered more or less from that bout of sickness; but from then onwards, it was only during the last four years of his life that he could at last escape from having his most hated word *invalid* slung at him whatever he most longed to do. Of course doctors always said, as doctors do, that he should lead 'a quiet life'; and perhaps there never was a less quiet life than that of R.L.S., from the time he cut himself off from his parents' help. His finances were in a desperate state by now, and he had to help Fanny too, but he would not write home for money, for he had heard nothing from his father or mother since the scrappy heart-broken note he wrote them when he first went on board the *Devonia*; and he believed they could not forgive him. To make things worse, when he started sending home chapters of *The Amateur Emigrant* for Sydney Colvin to try and get published and paid for, Colvin thought it poor stuff, and tactlessly wrote and told him so. Henley also wrote and let out that he felt much the same over *Travels with a Donkey*. It may be that both his close friends thought they could by these means get Louis to throw up his quest and come home, but he still held out, though inclined to lose his temper with their scoldings:

"Everybody writes me sermons; it's . . . hardly the food necessary for a man who lives all alone on forty-five cents a day, and sometimes less, with quantities of hard work and many heavy thoughts. If one of you could write me a letter with a jest in it—I am still flesh and blood——"

However, he loved Monterey and stayed there for several months. Just before Christmas he left, and went up to San Francisco hoping he might earn more there; for months he worked incredibly hard, ate far too little, and generally played tiddliwinks with his health, or rather with his lack of it; lived in a single room, fed at cheap restaurants on seventy cents a day, and would accept no money help: "This is a test; I *must* support myself," he said. Then he collapsed again and lay for weeks near to death; 'Death's Door' might indeed have been, on and off, one of his few permanent addresses. In a joking mood, he scribbled to Colvin a sketch of his tomb, and a poem for his epitaph which ended with the lines:

> Home is the sailor, home from sea,
> And the hunter home from the hill.

A joke's a joke—but it does not always remain so frightfully funny. . . . And little did he think— yes, we are at our old game again!—that this poem, with *Treasure Island*, would become the most popular thing he ever wrote, actually to be engraved at the side of his tomb on top of a mountain in Samoa.

Another acute illness knocked him out completely. Fanny helped the landlady nurse him, but without much hope that he could recover. When he was just able to stand again, a gaunt emaciated figure, he and Fanny at last were quietly married, but the doctor warned her that her husband could not live longer than a few months. But Fanny was a fighter too, and she kept him alive, or let's say she was his strong indomitable ally while he kept himself alive, for another fourteen years.

His luck turned; for his parents had heard of his plight and telegraphed him that he could count on £250 annually from them. 'You may imagine,' Louis wrote to Colvin, 'what a blessed business this was!'

After they were married, Louis and Fanny went up into the mountains north of San Francisco, to a mining town, deserted and ruined, called Silverado; reached by a wild drive in a six-horse coach whirling up the mountain, and then a climb on foot up a baked path running through a tangle of thick undergrowth. They took Lloyd with them, and lived in the old Silverado mine truck-house, surprisingly enjoying the experience. And as usual over everything he did and everywhere he went, Stevenson wrote a book about it called *The Silverado Squatters*.

Lloyd was now twelve, and his education could not be totally neglected. His young stepfather speaks somewhere of two hours daily nightmare known as 'Lloyd's lessons'. According to Lloyd's teacher, the boy then dashed up hallooing to a Chinaman's house where he had installed his toy printing-press . . . and Stevenson himself had to retire exhausted to his bed.

Louis' father and mother had begun to correspond with their new daughter-in-law, who wrote very affectionate letters full of details about their beloved son, his illnesses, his health, his occupations, always assuring them of his deep affection for them in spite of their long estrangement. But now the time was drawing near when they would have to meet, and they were all dreading it like a visit to the dentist—except Louis himself whose temperament was not likely to dread what seemed to him nothing more frightening than a happy meeting between the people he loved best on earth.

In August 1880, they sailed from New York, and were met at the Liverpool Docks by Thomas Stevenson and his gentle merry wife, and Sidney Colvin. Mr. Stevenson was not really formidable nor awe-inspiring, though Fanny must have expected all these attributes of a stern father-in-law. However, she won his heart in a quite unexpected way at their first meal in Edinburgh, at the house in Heriot Row. Probably because he was on the jump, or maybe because it was the accepted custom at that time to be less considerate of servants than it is now, he kept on scolding the maid who waited at table for various trifling mistakes. Suddenly, after the girl had left the room in tears, Fanny stood up, and looking Thomas Stevenson straight in the face, told him that if once again he behaved as badly to someone who couldn't answer back, she would leave the table and go straight up to her room. For a moment everybody must have trembled . . . then Thomas burst into a great roar of laughter: "I doot ye're a besom," he exclaimed, admiring her spirit, and from then she could do no wrong with 'Uncle Tom', as he bade her call him; she had made a complete conquest of him by her courage in taking such a colossal risk when she might have been pardoned for doing a little pretty 'sucking-up' instead.

Presently the whole family went up together to the Highlands which Louis loved; but the climate did not love him, and there was no doubt but that he had done himself serious damage by the hard conditions of over-work and semi-starvation which accompanied his rash rescuing journey to the woman with whom he had fallen so deeply in love. All the doctors agreed that he should spend the winter at Davos, high up in the mountains of Switzerland, where lung patients were being sent to recover or die. So Louis and Fanny and Lloyd went off at the end of October with a new member of their party, small and black, a Skye terrier given him by his friend Sir Walter Simpson, and named after the giver, Walter; which then, as dogs' names do, turned into Wattie, Woggie, Wogg, Woggin, Bogie and Bogue. Bogue was a gay excitable disobedient little fellow, and looking after him a three-man job; from the amused accounts of him, Stevenson may have been successful at many things he undertook, but not in the training of Wogg.

It was just as well he had something to amuse him, for in spite of his keen enjoyment of skating and tobogganing whenever he was well enough, he suffered from being shut up there in that big hotel in the snow. He and Lloyd got through a good many hours playing with soldiers on the boards of the hotel attic, though their absorption with mimic armies was really hardly a game at all, but miniature warfare. Luckily for them, nobody came in to say 'You must clear away all them soldiers before lunch', and they were often left spread over the chalked-out countries for days and weeks.

All the same, they were all glad when the spring released them from Davos. Lloyd had already been sent back to school in England; we never heard what he thought of this move towards getting him properly educated, whether he argued or was rather glad to get away from Davos; but it is certain that when he rejoined the whole family for the holidays, his mother and Lou, 'Uncle Tom' and 'Aunt Maggie', and of course Wogg, at a cottage they again rented in the Highlands, he was pretty bored by the perpetual Scottish rains that poured down all through that August; especially as Louis had an idea of putting in as candidate for the Edinburgh University Chair of History and Constitutional Law, and rehearsed his lectures on poor Lloyd. Polite and very weary, he did once wish aloud that his stepfather would "try and write something *interesting*", something that people like himself would enjoy reading. Instead of being offended by his devotee's criticism, R.L.S. burst out laughing, but perhaps held himself ready, if the chance occurred, to reward

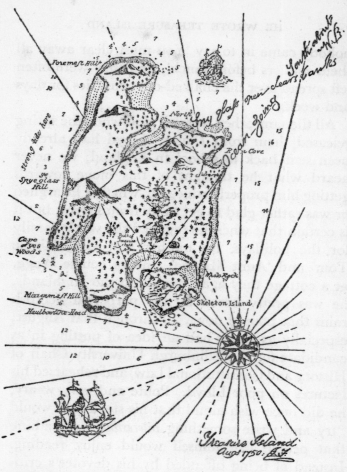

Treasure Island
Augt 1750. B.F

Given above J.F. & Mr W Bones Maite of yr Walrus
Savannah this twenty July 1754 W.B.

Facsimile of Chart; latitude and
longitude struck out by J. Hawkins

the boy both for listening so patiently to his lectures on Constitutional Law, and for having worked his way through every line of those 'horribly dull' books already written.

One windy rainy day in 'the late Miss Mac-Gregor's Cottage', as they always called it, having nothing better to do, Lloyd began idly drawing and painting the map of an imaginary island. Louis sauntered in, and also bored, leant over the young cartographer's shoulder . . . and thrilled as usual by anything to do with islands, ships and the sea, started to fill in the map with all sorts of thrilling names such as Spyglass Hill, Skeleton Island, Haulbowline Head and Mizzen-mast Hill. Then he made three red crosses: "that's where the treasure is buried", he replied airily to Lloyd's wildly eager questions; and wrote the words 'Treasure Island' in one corner; then put the map in his pocket and as though absentmindedly, walked off with it, possibly followed by shouts from Lloyd of "Hi, that's *my* map!"

The next morning Louis spent in bed; and sending for Lloyd, told him to "sit down and shut up" . . . Lloyd saw with wonder that his precious map was lying on the counterpane together with several sheets of manuscript. . . . And then Robert Louis Stevenson read aloud:

"Chapter I. The Old Sea-Dog at the 'Admiral Benbow'."

Never again did that particular schoolboy complain that his stepfather wrote only 'horribly dull books'. Here were Jim Hawkins and the Black Spot and Pew the scoundrelly blind beggar, here was the *Hispaniola* bound for the South Seas, and pirates and buried treasure and a parrot who had been taught to squawk 'Pieces of Eight', and Ben Gunn with his tangled beard, marooned for years on the island by cruel Captain Flint; here was the stockade and—oh well, you know now all about Treasure Island!

Naturally Lloyd was not to hear the whole book on the first day; it was not even called *Treasure Island* then; as we have already seen, Stevenson was rotten at titles, and he had called it *The Sea Cook*. Every evening, striding up and down the small stuffy sitting-room, he read aloud the chapters to the rest of the family and to whatever visitors happened to be staying with them; his cousin Etta was one; she was very old, over ninety, when I met her; but she had never forgotten the thrill of hearing Lou *act* it with his voice, and how

The Hispaniola from the Walt Disney film of *Treasure Island*
(reproduced by courtesy of *R.K.O. Radio Pictures Ltd.*)

delighted her Uncle Tom had been. He it was who named Flint's old ship: *The Walrus*, and helped Louis provide the correct bloodthirsty contents of Billy Brown's chest:

"A quadrant, a tin cannikin, several sticks of tobacco, two brace of very handsome pistols, a piece of bar silver, an old Spanish watch and some other trinkets of little value and mostly of foreign make, a pair of compasses mounted with brass, and five or six curious West Indian shells . . ."

It was hardly surprising for Lloyd to feel that *Treasure Island* was very especially *his* book, which but for him would never have been written. He pleaded that there should be no women in it; rightly or wrongly maintaining that they spoilt the story; Stevenson laughed and obeyed, though he made an exception of Jim Hawkins' mother who was necessary for the first few chapters before Jim, Squire Trelawney and the doctor set sail in the *Hispaniola*, innocent of having signed on among their crew a whole gang of buccaneers, led by the smooth-tongued crippled sea-cook, Long John Silver. . . .

Finally (and this must have been a tremendous

moment for the boy) when *Treasure Island* was published, it was dedicated:—

TO

LLOYD OSBOURNE

An American Gentleman

In accordance with whose classic taste

The following narrative has been designed

It is now, in return for numerous delightful hours

And with the kindest wishes, dedicated

by his affectionate friend

THE AUTHOR

It did not appear at once bound in volume form, but ran through *Young Folks* as a serial, and funnily enough, was not very popular with its young readers then; they much preferred another serial Stevenson wrote later, not half so good, called *The Black Arrow*; which was dedicated to Fanny for an amusing reason, exactly the opposite from why he dedicated *Treasure Island* to Lloyd: secretly he used to watch her trying again and again to work her way through it, but never able to get beyond the first few pages. So in his dedication he wrote:

CRITIC ON THE HEARTH

. . I have watched with interest, with pain, and at length with amusement, your unavailing attempts to peruse *The Black Arrow*; and I think I should lack humour indeed, if I let the occasion slip and did not place your name in the fly-leaf of the only book of mine that you have never read —and never will read.

Richard III came into this historical tale (which Louis himself called 'tushery') as a hunchback boy called Dickon, and this character is the best thing in the book. One critical young reader wrote to Stevenson after the last instalment of *The Black Arrow* had appeared as a serial, pointing out carefully that there had been *four* arrows to be used with deadly intent; and though three had been accounted for in the concluding instalment, the fourth was not even mentioned: 'nor is there any indication of the fate of Sir Oliver, for whom the fourth arrow was evidently intended.' He received at once the delighted reply from the author: 'Thanks to you, sir, he shall die the death.'

When at last in 1883 *Treasure Island* was accepted as a book, the publisher offered him a

hundred pounds, and Stevenson wrote home
exultantly from Hyères to announce the great
news:

"There has been offered for *Treasure Island*—
how much do you suppose? I believe it would be
an excellent jest to keep the answer till my next
letter. For two cents I would do so. Shall I?
Anyway, I'll turn the page first. No—well—A
hundred pounds, all alive, O! A hundred jingling,
tingling, golden, minted quid. Is not this wonderful? . . . it does look as if I should support myself
without trouble in the future. If I have only
health, I can, I thank God. It is dreadful to be a
great, big man, and not be able to buy bread."

Little-did-he-think that only about ten years
later, a little while before he died in the South
Seas, his friends were arranging for a Collected
Edition of his works to appear, the Edinburgh
Edition, which they assured him would bring him
in at least £5000 to start with, so that he could
relax and take it easy and enjoy a holiday free
from writing for a little while. But he could not
believe it even then; and he was never to take a
holiday from writing. For one thing, he remem-

bered all his life how illness had made it necessary for him, while still a beginner, to take money from his father in order to support his 'family', and he could not bear the idea of ever having to do so again. As he had no children of his own, he always liked to think of Fanny's children, Lloyd and Belle, as his family, and Belle's little son, Austin. He certainly loved them as though they were indeed his own, and used to have enormous fun playing with them, not just pretending to enjoy it but as keen and absorbed as they were themselves.

Lloyd was astoundingly lucky in his companion during these years, and knew it (which does not always follow); for after that cold and rainy summer in the Highlands, Stevenson was once more banished to Davos for the winter, and this time they did not live in the hotel, but took a small châlet near-by. There, again kneeling on the attic floor, they directed and fought their campaigns as General Stevenson and General Osbourne, hurling defiance at one another while they disposed their armies of toy soldiers. Stevenson ran a newspaper supposed to be by imaginary War Correspondents on both sides, as near as possible to the actual scene of battle. This paper was called the *Yallobally Record*, hot as ginger and violently abusive. Lloyd has confessed that although he pretended to laugh at the columns of the *Yallobally Record*, actually they upset him terribly, and that it was a relief when Louis (perhaps guessing its effect on his sensitive stepson) gave him permission to 'suppress its publication, and hang the editor'. Here is a quotation from the *Yallobally Record* which shows us exactly what Lloyd means:

"We have never concealed our opinion that Osbourne was a bummer and a scallywag; but the entire collapse of his campaign beats the worst that we imagined possible. We have received, at the same moment, news of Green and La Fayette's column being beaten ignominiously back again across the Sandusky river and out of Grierson, a place on our own side; and next day of the appearance of a large body of troops at Yolo, in the very heart of this great land, where they seem to have played the very devil, taking prisoners by the hundred and marching with arrogant footsteps on the sacred soil of the province of Savannah, General Napoleon, the only commander who has not yet disgraced himself, still fights an uphill battle in the centre, inflicting terrific losses and upholding the honour of his country single-handed. The infamous Osbourne is shaking in his spectacles at Savannah. He was roundly taken to task by a public-spirited reporter, and babbled meaningless excuses; he did not know, he said, that the force now falling in on us at Yolo was so large. It was his business to know. What is he paid for? That large force has been ten days at least on our own side of the frontier. Where were Osbourne's wits? Will it be believed, the column at Lone Bluff is again short of ammunition? This old man of the sea, whom all the world knows to be an ass and whom we can prove to be a coward, is apparently a peculator also. If we were to die tomorrow, the word 'Osbourne' would be found engraven backside foremost on our hearts."

They took Lloyd's toy printing-press out to Davos, as well as the armies of toy soldiers, and with it he set out to earn some money to help along the family funds; for he happened to over-hear Louis say to Fanny between bouts of a racking cough: "It's no good, Fanny, we shall have to write to my father again"—and the boy knew well enough from his voice how he hated doing that. Lloyd was no prig; he enjoyed the winter sports, tobogganing and skating, with all his might; but he was the sort of boy who got worried when people he loved were in trouble; and moreover he had an idea that his own upkeep and education were a pretty fair expense. So he struck a bargain with the manager of the hotel to print the hundred programmes needed every week for their Saturday concerts. This black-bearded gentleman was very formidable in the matter of spelling, and Lloyd once had to reprint the entire batch because of one trifling mistake that anyone might have made in the title of a song, ' 'Twas in *Trofolgar's* Bay'. He also printed the announcements for charity bazaars, public notices, letterheads and so forth; and Blackbeard was at least punctual over payments. R.L.S. from the start obviously longed to share in working the printing-press; and wrote a poem for it, a 'Martial Elegy for some Lead Soldiers', wherein he mourned for their dear Captain's sake:

> Who saw his heroes shed their gore,
> And lacked a shilling to buy more!

Lloyd grew more ambitious; he wrote and printed a small book called *Black Canyon or Life in the Far West*, with illustrations that were wood-cuts made from the blocks already supplied with the printing-press. He sold them for sixpence each; and if you have the luck to find a copy stuck away among a pile of old books, you can now get at least £25 for it.

At last R.L.S. could no longer bear to be shut out of all this activity, and Lloyd relates how Louis called one day at the Editorial Offices and with deep humility 'submitted' a manuscript of poems; after what would probably have been some lordly parleying, the youthful editor accepted and published it; he sold out the whole edition of fifty copies, so was able to pay his contributor three francs in royalties—"The only successful book I've ever written," remarked Robert Louis Stevenson, delightedly spinning his coins in the air. In a letter to a friend in England, however, he wrote a different story: 'I declare I'm ruined. I got a penny a cut and a halfpenny a set of verses from the flint-hearted publisher, and only one specimen copy.'

Their longings began to soar to the heights. Lloyd had used up all his ready-made woodcuts for *Black Canyon*, but they had to have illustrations for their future work; so Louis got some thin wood and carved pictures on it with a pocket-knife.

The first proof was a sickening disappointment because the impression was unequal. Then Fanny had the really brilliant notion of building it up with cigarette-papers. They found a Swiss invalid in the village to reproduce a dozen blocks, and,

breathlessly excited, printed ninety copies of *Moral Emblems: A Collection of Cuts and Verses*, price sixpence. Encouraged by its sensational sales, they followed it up with a *Second Collection of Moral Emblems*, all very impudent and funny, showing the awful fate that befell certain people who were not careful what they did:[1]

1. The picture on this page and page 96 are reproductions of the original woodcuts.

The Abbot for a walk went out,
A wealthy cleric, very stout,
And Robin has that Abbot stuck
As the red hunter spears the buck.
The djavel or the javelin
Has, you observe, gone bravely in,
And you may hear that weapon whack
Bang through the middle of his back.
Hence we may learn that Abbots should
Never go walking in a wood.

'The Pirate and the Apothecary', a much
longer poem, had several fine illustrations, but a
somewhat doubtful moral:

Come, lend me an attentive ear
A startling moral tale to hear,
Of Pirate Rob and Chemist Ben,
And different destinies of men . . .

Together but unlike they grew;
Robin was tough, and through and through
Bold, inconsiderate, and manly,
Like some historic Bruce or Stanley.

Ben had a mean and servile soul,
He robbed not, though he often stole;

95

He sang on Sunday in the choir,
And tamely capped the passing Squire . . .

The master of a trading dandy
Hires Robin for a go of brandy;
And all the happy hills of Rome
Vanish beyond the fields of foam.

Ben, meanwhile, like a tin reflector,
Attended on the worthy rector;
Opened his eyes and held his breath,
And flattered to the point of death;

96

And was at last, by that good fairy,
Apprenticed to the Apothecary . . .
At length, from years of anxious toil,
Bold Robin seeks his native soil   . .

. . . Ben told the tale of his indentures,
And Rob narrated his adventures.
Last, as the point of greatest weight,
The pair contrasted their estate.
And Robin, like a boastful sailor,
Despised the other for a tailor.

'See,' he remarked, 'with envy see
A man with such a fist as me!
Bearded and ringed, and big, and brown,
I sit and toss the stingo down.
Hear the gold jingle in my bag—
All won beneath the Jolly Flag!'

. . . The smiling chemist tapped his brow.
'Rob,' he replied, 'this throbbing brain
Still worked and hankered after gain;
By day and night, to work my will,
It pounded like a powder mill;
And marking how the world went round
A theory of theft it found.

97

Here is the key to right and wrong:
Steal little but steal all day long.'

We can imagine what fun Lloyd and Louis had with the printing-press, quite apart from the thrill of local fame at Davos, and heaping up riches by their 'phenomenal sales'. During a summer holiday when Lloyd was older, they started again, but the printing-press broke down and could not be repaired.

Naturally Stevenson had to be doing his own grown-up writing too, whenever he was well enough (and often when he wasn't); but after another summer in Scotland, he decided not to go back to Switzerland and the high snows. They went instead to live on the Mediterranean shore of France, and took a little villa at Hyères called *Chalet la Solitude*, where they lived for the next sixteen months. He always said afterwards that this was the happiest time of his life, when he felt that at last he had a home of his own. Not that he was well the whole time he was there—far from it; twice he nearly died of a hæmorrhage and had to remain for ages in bed, the room darkened because of his eyes, forbidden to talk louder than a whisper, and with his right arm strapped down so that he should not move it and have a heart attack. Once when he was carried home unable to speak because his mouth was full of blood, and Fanny was trying with a shaking hand to pour out a dose of his emergency medicine, he made a sign that he wanted a writing-block and pencil, and wrote on it to reassure her, in perfectly firm, small hand-writing: 'Don't worry, if this is death it is very easy.' Stevenson may have longed all his life to be a soldier, and chafed that the career should have been denied him because of the tricks his lungs played him at the slightest exertion; but though he enjoyed a bit of outward swagger and bravado, by nature he was a humble man with a small opinion of himself, and had no idea that in the hero sense of the word, he *was* a soldier and a good soldier too.

Somehow, then, he managed to remain cheerful; and it was at this time that he wrote most of those gay jingles in *A Child's Garden of Verses*, though nobody who read them could ever have thought they were written while he lay flat and helpless in the semi-darkness. And he wrote quantities of nonsense letters to his friends and family, full of ridiculous verses, and complaining loudly that they did not write to him often enough.

In one letter he says: "Why am I so penniless, ever, ever penniless, ever, ever penny-penny-less and dry? The birds upon the thorn, the poppies in the corn, they surely are more fortunate or prudenter than I!" And in another:

"I had intended to spend my life (or any leisure I might have from Piracy upon the high seas) as the leader of a great horde of irregular cavalry, devastating whole valleys. I can still, looking back, see myself in many favourite attitudes; signalling for a boat from my pirate ship with a pocket-handkerchief, I at the jetty end, and one or two of my bold blades keeping the crowd at bay; or else turning in my saddle to look back at my whole command (some five thousand strong) following me at the hand-gallop up the road out of the burning valley: this last by moonlight."

Stevenson and his father were by now tremendous friends, and Thomas Stevenson fretted a lot at the absence of his only son; so in 1885 Louis and Fanny came back and settled down in a house on the cliff in Bournemouth, which they called *Skerryvore*. It was given by the old man to his daughter-in-law as a very special present, and they lived there for three years—"like a weevil in a biscuit", Stevenson remarked furiously, for it turned out that Bournemouth did not suit him and he was ill all the time, doing most of his writing in bed. Some very good stuff all the same came out of that bedroom; *Kidnapped* for instance —David Balfour and Alan Breck became as well-known as Jim Hawkins and Long John Silver; not many battles on land or sea have been described with as swinging zest as the Siege in the Round-house: David and Alan with their backs to the wall, two against fifteen, taking on the treacherous crew of s.s. *Covenant*.

Towards the end of the Bournemouth period, he wrote the book which was to have enormous sales and set him free from money worries for a long time. One can still see it quoted all over the place, over and over and over again, about twenty times a week, whenever anybody wants to call attention to the fact that most human beings have two sides to them, a good and a bad; sometimes one side gets uppermost and sometimes the other. Stevenson had once informed Andrew Lang that he meant to write a story 'about a fellow who was two fellows'—and this book was called *The Strange Case of Dr. Jekyll and Mr. Hyde*. He wrote it at top

speed in three days, because they were very broke
again, unable to pay their tradesmen's bills, and
he said he could always hear the wheels of Byles-
the-butcher's cart going through his mind whenever he tried to think of anything more profitable.
A friend advised him to write a 'Shilling Shocker',
as they were called then; nowadays it would
probably be referred to as a 'Whodunit'. One
night he was making an awful row, calling out and
tossing in his sleep, so Fanny woke him; he
exclaimed wrathfully: "You shouldn't have woken
me, I was dreaming a fine bogey tale," and while
he still remembered it, down it went. When it
was finished, he showed it to Fanny with some
pride, but she was an honest woman and said it
would not do, he had written it just as a bogey
tale and what really counted in it was the allegory,
its 'underneath' meaning. Louis had a hot temper
and one imagines that he swore at first, in his disappointment at not getting the sweet praise he
thought he deserved. But later, when Fanny was
downstairs, she heard him violently ringing his
bell, and going up to see what he wanted, there
he was, leaning back exhausted against his pillows,
coughing and unable to speak, pointing with a
long, skinny finger to a spiral of smoke rising from

a pile of paper burning in the grate. . . . He had come to the conclusion that Fanny was right in what she said. She flew to rescue the manuscript: "Surely *some* of it can still be used?" but he declared that would be no good, he would be tempted to use too much. He then rewrote the whole thing in another three days.

Everything about Jekyll and Hyde was unexpected; for when it was published, it made a huge success *not* as a 'shocker' but because all up and down the country, beginning with St. Paul's Cathedral, sermons were preached about it from the pulpit, saying what a grand lesson it taught.

Success at last!

Thomas Stevenson died about a year later, and then Louis decided to give up the house at Bournemouth and to visit America. He was getting restless, and he thought, quite rightly, that it was about time Fanny and Lloyd had a chance to visit their own relations in their own country. His mother decided to come too, and their faithful French *bonne*, Valentine Roche, who had followed them from Hyères to look after them at *Skerryvore*. Once again his close friends, Henley, Colvin, Mrs. Sitwell, Henry James and many others, had to say good-bye to Louis; and this time, though

none of them knew it, when s.s. *Ludgate Hill*
carried off the little party from the Royal Albert
Docks, they had seen him for the last time.

It carried off, besides their little party, a very
odd cargo. The man of the family had been left
to choose the boat and get the tickets, and it was
not till they were aboard that they realised Louis
had carelessly booked their passages in a ship with
a freight of apes, stallions and matches. Not that
he himself minded; he was a grand sailor and did
not like ordinary conventional travelling; at once
he struck up a friendship with one of the baboons,
who would go about everywhere on his shoulder,
and whose embrace, he wrote home to Colvin,
nearly cost him a coat. But poor Fanny was a
bad sailor, and this trip was the beginning of her
long gallant endurances during the next six years,
under wretched conditions, and through every
sort of gale and wild seas. Her great comfort,
however, was to see 'my two boys' (meaning
Louis and Lloyd) having the time of their lives.
Since most of our heroes have faults, I should say
that R.L.S., though instantly and swiftly ready
to help anybody in trouble, was Prince Inconsiderate in his ordinary daily life; and Fanny's sea-
sickness did not prevent him from setting out

light-heartedly on long voyages to the most in-accessible coasts and islands in the world, in battered old boats, through squalls and hurri-canes, happily ignoring privation and danger and horrid discomfort. Of course you might argue that there was no need for *her* to go at all; he would never have *dragged* her along; but then he and Fanny were greatly devoted, and always did things together. Except for her sea-sickness, which nobody can help, hers was a bold and valiant spirit, and she certainly would not have let her irrepressible husband go off and get into mischief on his own. She was twelve years older than he, and because of his brittle lungs, felt naturally more protective than an ordinary wife. I am sure she would have said that her favourite photograph of him was a snapshot taken on board the *Equator*, a schooner bound for the Gilbert Islands; for it must have been a joyous moment for her anxious heart, always strained and fearful when he had to be cooped up, to see him at last as tough as other men, clinging to the rigging and jubilantly spear-ing fish.

Actually, by far the best of his photos is the one where he is shown sitting at his desk in Bourne-mouth, and suddenly looks up as though a deep

H

thought had struck him. . . . What really made
him look up was a schoolboy opening the door of
his study, breaking the law that no one was to
interrupt while he was writing like blazes and
trying to concentrate. R.S.L. barked: "O-U-T
out!" and Lloyd fled—(the story comes direct from
his elder sister)—but not before he had clicked
the shutter of his camera. There are dozens of
photographs and paintings and portraits of R.L.S.;
and the most detestable show him with long
untidy hair lapping the shoulders of the velvet
coat he nearly always wore, and a wistful, sweet,
far-away expression; but we need take no notice
of these; his mother preferred them, naturally;
mothers like their sons to look romantic; but
Louis was anything but sweet and wistful and far-
away; or at least, when he *was* far away, his body,
well or ill, had always gone with him and was up
to every sort of audacious enterprise likely to
drive his friends and doctors and nurses and
family half mad with anxiety. Anyhow, Belle
says that 'O-U-T *out*' is more like him than any
other photograph ever taken, and she ought to
know. The one he liked best himself, though he
laughed at all of them, was a portrait painted by
a Count Nerli when he was in the South Seas; it

R.L.S. from a snapshot taken by Lloyd Osbourne

Stevenson's house at Vailima

gave him a lean piratical look, and his mother did not care for it at all!

Anyhow, whenever Stevenson was at sea, he was more pirate than author, rejoicing to have escaped at last from his invalid life. He wrote to Colvin:

"O, it was lovely on our stable-ship, chock full of stallions. She rolled heartily, rolled some of the fittings out of our state-room, and I think a more dangerous cruise (except that it was summer) it would be hard to imagine. But we enjoyed it to the masthead, all but Fanny; and even she perhaps a little."

(one is inclined to doubt that last happy-go-lucky statement.)

Their arrival in New York showed that R.L.S. had now become a celebrity: for two little pilot boats were sent out to meet the S.S. *Ludgate Hill* and bring her in; and one of the pilots, the pleasant one, had been nicknamed Jekyll, and the other, a surly brute, was always known among his comrades as Hyde.

CHAPTER FIVE

OF course R.L.S. overdid it in New York, and
enjoyed being fêted, and became an easy
prey to enthusiastic lion-hunters, and was offered
staggering sums of money for about three-and-a-
half lines of his writing, and had a tiresome
collapse and was put to bed and overdid it there
too. So they were sent off by the doctors to the
top of another mountain draped in snow and ice;
not Davos this time, but Saranac in the Adirondacks. The hut where they lived was run by a
kindly frontiersman and his wife; and with pride
for many years afterwards they showed reverential
pilgrims their relics of a careless but engaging
patient who burnt holes with his cigarettes in *all*
their sheets, and still managed to get away with
it.

Saranac was so cold that Stevenson said if they
hung the thermometer in the porch, the quicksilver rushed down to the bottom of the bulb and
curled up and lay hibernating like a bear. When

he had procured a buffalo robe and leggings, so he wrote to his old friend Will Low, the latter might then come and stay with him, but not before, in case Low should want to paint him as a plain man, which he was not—'but a rank Saranacker and wild man of the woods'. Here, with Lloyd collaborating as gaily as six years ago in *Moral Emblems*, he wrote that rollicking tale: *The Wrong Box*; and also started a grim grand novel: *The Master of Ballantrae*, because the view from their log cabin reminded him desperately of Scotland; and he was to long for Scotland all the rest of his life as an exile. 'All the rest of his life' was now to be only six years, but they were at least, and in spite of homesickness, splendid active years crammed with adventure; to which cat-boat sailing could be added when his mountain cure was over and he went down to stay with friends on the New Jersey coast.

And soon he was going to change his address again in a big way—(that man was for ever pretending to settle down and then tearing up roots anew, yet he had the cheek to say that he struck his friends from his correspondence list directedly *they* changed their address more than *once*!). It must have been a glorious sensation to have for address: 'On board the *Casco*, the Pacific Ocean'; for to possess a yacht of his own had always been his sort of 'pony dream'; I doubt if we would ever have found the usual pony appearing on his juvenile Christmas list; though when he reached his final address, the one that had never to be crossed out: Robert Louis Stevenson, Vailima, near Apia, Upolu, Samoa, South Pacific, he *did* have a pony, and rode on it to a paper-chase on the plantation, and came in third:

". . . It is really better fun than following the hounds, since you have to be your own hound, and a precious bad hound I was, following every false scent on the whole course to the bitter end; but I came in third at the last on my little Jack, who stuck to it gallantly."

And in another letter, he breaks into doggerel inspired by 'The misconduct of his little raving lunatic of an old beast of a pony'—

There was racing and chasing in Vailele planta-
   tion,
And vastly we enjoyed it,
But alas! for the state of my foundation,
For it wholly has destroyed it!

But that is looking ahead; and meanwhile there will be some spell-binding addresses to put on our list: Papeete, Tautira, Honolulu, the Gilbert Islands. The *Casco* was not exactly his own yacht; with the legacy his father left him, he chartered it at San Francisco to go on a long cruise in the South Seas; made possible by the editor of an American magazine who came to stay with him at Saranac, and heard him long to get away from the bitter cold and the white frozen weather into real tropical sunshine. Mr. McClure then suggested that if Louis cared to go on a voyage to the Pacific and visit its archipelago of islands, they would publish his diary of the cruise. *If* he cared to?—R.L.S., of course, fell in love with the idea and decided to risk the yacht; he was beginning to make quite a lot of money with his articles in America; they lapped up anything he sent them, though sometimes he refused what he thought were fantastically high prices, saying his stuff was not worth it, which must have surprised the editors *very* much.

So on June 15th, 1888, the *Casco* steamed through the Golden Gates with Louis and Fanny and Lloyd, Valentine Roche, and that really valiant old lady, Mrs. Thomas Stevenson, who

remained quite tranquil in spite of the violent
changes that had taken place in her life from
when she was a demure daughter of the Manse at
Colinton. The captain of the yacht was rather on
Mrs. Stevenson's mind, for he did not attend any
of the prayer services which she insisted should be
held regularly. Once, dramatically, he struck the
mast with his fist to prove some argument of
unbelief, and the mast was rotten. They might
otherwise never have found it out till they were
at sea again and perhaps in a squall, and that
would have meant the end of the yacht and of all
on board.

Apparently it proved a perilous voyage to the
Marquesas, and then to the Tahiti group, and
finally through 40 degrees of latitude to Honolulu
and the Sandwich Islands:

> O, how my spirit languishes
> To step ashore on the Sanguishes

he scribbled home to Colvin, in what could not
have been one of his noblest poems. And in
another letter, hardly less flippantly:

"We are speeding along through a nasty swell,
and I can only keep my place at the table by

means of a foot against the divan, the unoccupied hand meanwhile gripping the ink-bottle."

The *Casco* was a graceful luxurious schooner; the South Sea islanders called her the Silver Ship, but she was over-rigged and over-sparred. Louis was in his element all the time: "This is the life for a man like me, this is the life for ever!" He hit it off tremendously well with cannibal kings and tall warriors and tattooed Polynesian queens. The climate, too, was wonderful; nights under the Southern stars, as warm as milk; and his health stood up to it all splendidly; he developed a huge appetite, and reports arrogantly how at one native feast in his honour, he sent up his plate four times for more pig. They ate raw fish with sauce made of coconut milk mixed with sea-water and lime-juice, taro poi-poi, and bananas roasted in hot stones in a little pit in the ground, with coconut cream to eat with them. That sort of food! And lived almost entirely in the open air, as nearly without clothes as possible, and certainly without shoes and stockings, wading for hours in shallow water, looking for shells; except Mrs. Thomas Stevenson who consented to leave off her stockings, but as a concession to Edinburgh standards, trotted round in neat sandals, and always firmly wore her widow's cap, looking like portraits of Queen Victoria with the addition of a wreath of gaudy exotic flowers hung round her neck. When they were invited to local feasts on the islands, especially those given by the beautiful brown princess Moë, they all wore wreaths of golden leaves on their heads, which was apparently the correct thing to do.

Their favourite place was Tautira, where the Chief, Ori, became one of Louis' special friends, and invited them to stay for two months in his house, while the *Casco* with her rotten mast went to be made seaworthy again. Stevenson's letters home were full of Ori, what a splendid fellow he was, like a Colonel of the Guards, how they had swopped names (a compliment and mark of great affection) and Ori became Rui, as near as he could get to Louis, and Louis 'Teriitera', Ori's Christian name.

The king of Honolulu, too, Kalakua, became Louis' close pal, and they frequently drank champagne together, His Majesty's favourite tipple. The feminine members of the party, while all this male hobnobbing was going on, learnt hat-making, a special accomplishment of the

ladies out there; Fanny said that if you wanted to
pay a compliment to another lady, you gave her
a hat; she and her mother-in-law had at least
thirteen such compliments.

After they sailed away from Tautira, Ori a Ori
wrote them a very touching farewell letter:

"I make you to know my great affection. When
you embarked I felt a great sorrow. It is for this
that I went upon the road, and you looked from
that ship, and I looked at you on the ship with
great grief until you had raised the anchor and
hoisted the sails. When the ship started, I ran
along the beach to see you still; and when you
were on the open sea I cried out to you, 'farewell
Louis': and when I was coming back to my house
I seemed to hear your voice crying 'Rui farewell'.
Afterwards I watched the ship as long as I could
until the night fell . . . I did not sleep that night,
thinking continually of you, my very dear friend,
until the morning. . . . Afterwards I looked into
your rooms; they did not please me as they used
to do. . . . Rising up I went to the beach to see
your ship, and I could not see it. . . . I will not
forget you in my memory. Here is the thought:
I desire to meet you again. It is my dear Teriitera

makes the only riches I desire in this world. . . .
But now we are separated. May God be with you
all."

Louis was always saying he had not enough
time to write his numberless duty and business
letters, but on the other hand, just for the fun of
it, he sometimes scribbled home a letter of vivid
description to 'Tomarcher', the son of William
Archer; which was a bit of a waste, for Tomarcher
was then only three:

Dear Tomarcher,—This is a pretty state of
things! seven o'clock and no word of breakfast!
And I was awake a good deal last night, for it was
full moon, and they had made a great fire of coconut husks down by the sea, and as we have no
blinds or shutters, this kept my room very bright.
And then the rats had a wedding or a school-
feast under my bed. . . . This is a much better
place for children than any I have hitherto seen
in these seas. The girls (and sometimes the boys)
play a very elaborate kind of hopscotch. The
boys play horses exactly as we do in Europe; and
have very good fun on stilts, trying to knock each
other down, in which they do not often succeed.

The children of all ages go to church and are allowed to do what they please, running about the aisles, rolling balls, stealing mamma's bonnet and publicly sitting on it, and at last going to sleep in the middle of the floor. I forgot to say that the whips to play horses, and the balls to roll about the church—at least I never saw them used elsewhere—grow ready-made on trees; which is rough on toy-shops. The whips are so good that I wanted to play horses myself; but no such luck! my hair is grey, and I am a great, big, ugly man.

. . . I used to be the best player of hide-and-seek going; not a good runner, I was up to every shift and dodge, I could jink very well, I could crawl without any noise through leaves, I could hide under a carrot plant, it used to be my favourite boast that I always *walked* into the den. . . .

The children beat their parents here; it does not make their parents any better; so do not try it.

R.L.S. was good at writing to children; and another letter he was later to write to the little daughter of Chief Justice Ide, on Samoa, became known all over the world. He happened to learn that Annie Ide had always complained about her hard luck in having a birthday on Christmas Day.

Instantly sympathetic—for what was the fun of getting only one day of presents and spoiling when more fortunate children had two?—he wrote offering to mend matters by swopping birthdays with her; and enclosed a solemn legal document setting forth her now undisputed claim to take over November 13th for her own. If at any time she had no further use for it, he said, it was to go to the President of the United States. Annie H. Ide lived to be an old lady and used a long string of her borrowed birthdays; she died quite recently, and the President of the United States then quoted this document to establish his formal right of inheritance:

I, Robert Louis Stevenson, Advocate of the Scots Bar . . . and considering that I, the said Robert Louis Stevenson, have attained an age when O, we never mention it . . . *have transferred*, and do hereby transfer, to the said Annie H. Ide, *all and whole* my rights and privileges in the thirteenth day of November, formerly my birthday, and hereby and henceforth, the birthday of the said Annie H. Ide, to have, hold, exercise, and enjoy the same, in the customary manner, by the sporting of fine raiment, eating of rich meats, and receipt of gifts, compliments, and copies of verse, according to the manner of our ancestors. . .

Not that Stevenson could complain of his birthday celebrations once he had become the High Chief Tusitala at Vailima. 'O-we-never-mention-it'?—Well, his stepdaughter described a native feast at which, in addition to a pile of rich and mostly edible presents, he was given yet another fine new name:

"We had sixteen pigs roasted whole underground, three enormous fish (small whales, Lloyd called them), 400 pounds of salt beef, ditto of pork, 200 heads of taro, great bunches of bananas, native delicacies done up in bundles of ti leaves, 800 pineapples, many weighing 15 pounds, all from Lloyd's patch, oranges, tinned salmon, sugar-cane, and ship's biscuit in proportion. Among the presents to Tusitala, besides flowers and wreaths, were fans, native baskets, rolls of tapa, ava bowls, coconut cups beautifully polished, and a talking-man's staff; and one pretty girl from Tanugamanono appeared in a fine mat (the diamonds and plate of Samoa), which she wore over her simple tapa kilt, and laid at Tusitala's feet when she departed. Seumanu, the high chief of Apia, presented Louis with the title of 'Au-mai-taua-i-manu-vao.' "

While they were all living at Honolulu, Stevenson went over to visit the leper settlement on the island of Molokai, and was deeply impressed at what had been done for the lepers by a brave priest, Father Damien, who had come to settle among them and done so much by his labours to change the island from an unendurable place of desolation and misery to an abode where amazing hope and courage and cheerfulness could be found. But at last came a tragic day when the priest started his sermon, not with his usual: "My dear brethren," but with "Fellow lepers". . . . And then they knew that he had caught the dreaded disease.

When Stevenson arrived, they were still mourning the death of Father Damien, and so he heard a great deal about him. General Gordon of Khartoum had always been one of his heroes, and now he had another saint and hero to put beside him. He stayed a week at Molokai, and made himself useful yarning with old blind leper beachcombers in the hospital, or rode over to the

Convent and played croquet with the leper children, refusing to wear gloves; he had replied to Fanny when she begged him to take a pair along for safety's sake: "They have enough to bear without that!" When he returned to Honolulu he sent them a grand piano, and also wrote to his friends in England asking them to send scraps for doll dressmaking to the Reverend Sister Maryanne at Molokai, because the little girls all had dolls and loved dressing them.

His stay on the island had, however, more sensational results than the parcels of brocade, silk and velvet that were sped across the Atlantic and the Pacific oceans. Nearly a year later, when Stevenson was in Sydney and, as he thought, dawdling back at last to Scotland, he happened to see in a newspaper what we should call a simply beastly letter from the Bishop of Honolulu about Father Damien, vetoing the idea of putting up a statue to him because of his few very pardonable human faults and failings during the years of his exile on Molokai. Whereupon Stevenson lost his temper in a big way. And when he did let fly in a righteous cause, people remembered it. They have had reason to remember this particular burst of rage for more than sixty years, for one of the most magnificent things he ever wrote was his Open Letter in Defence of Father Damien, addressed to the smug and sanctimonious bishop. Of course it was longer than letters usually are, because he had a great deal to say on the subject, and said it eloquently and without mincing his words at all. When he had finished, he read it aloud to Fanny and Belle and Lloyd, because they were his family and therefore had a right to be consulted before he sent it to be published anywhere; for it was probable that the Bishop would bring a successful libel case against him, and that would mean a loss of all the money they had assembled with such difficulty, and they would have to start again from the beginning. But when they had heard the letter, his family felt exactly the same as he did, and cried enthusiastically in chorus: "Publish it! publish it!"

There was no libel case. And thanks to Robert Louis Stevenson, Father Damien will now always be remembered as sacrificing his life and more than his life to help the lepers.

CHAPTER SIX

"RAIN, calms, squalls, bang—there's the fore-topmast gone; rain, calm, squalls, away with the stay-sail; more rain, more calm, more squalls; a prodigious heavy sea all the time, and the *Equator* staggering and hovering like a swallow in a storm; and the cabin, a great square, crowded with wet human beings, and the rain avalanching on the deck, and the leaks dripping everywhere: Fanny, in the midst of fifteen males, bearing up wonderfully."

Bearing up wonderfully, indeed. For their next Pacific voyage could not have been more unlike their first experience in a millionaire's yacht, the Silver Ship, now sent back to its owner in San Francisco. On board the *Casco* they had had tribulations, certainly; but Fanny must have thought of it as a yacht from Paradise, looking back on it from her inferno on board the *Equator*, a trading schooner bound for the Gilbert Islands and the Marshalls. All the same, to see Louis so well and active and happy, thriving on danger, was to her worth any sacrifice; and though Lloyd showed hankerings now and then for a University and a scholarly life, he too found knocking about among the South Sea Islands not too dull a substitute. So their friends in England and Scotland had to resign themselves to the idea of not seeing the fugitives from civilisation for several months more. Waiting for a suitable ship to slide past the reef and into the lagoon, they camped out at Apemama; and Fanny planted some onions and radishes which actually came up, a rare thing on these low islands; Louis declared that his heart would leap at the sight of a coster's barrow and he would shed tears over a dish of turnips. While Fanny was gardening, he amused himself by striking up yet another unconventional friendship with royalty. His letters about His Majesty King Tembinoka might easily have been written in the mischievous hope of somewhat shocking his close friend, Sidney Colvin, now Curator of the British Museum; for instance, when he prattles innocently of a charming murderer:

". . . in his big home out of a wreck, with his

New Hebrides wife in her savage turban of hair and yet a perfect lady, and his three adorable little girls in Rob Roy MacGregor dresses, dancing to the hand organ, performing circus on the floor . . . and curling up together on a mat to sleep, three sizes, three attitudes, three Rob Roy dresses, and six little clenched fists: the murderer meanwhile brooding and gloating over his chicks, till your whole heart went out to him."

And Louis was apparently not the only one of their party to 'take people as they came' in the tropics, whose doings might have roused a mild protest in Europe. Years afterwards, Fanny told some friends how Louis' mother had actually taken walks with a native chieftain who had killed thousands and eaten hundreds. "Oh, *Fanny!*" Mrs. Thomas Stevenson exclaimed in horror at such exaggeration. "You *know* it was only eleven!"

When they gave up the *Casco*, Louis' mother decided to take a rest from cannibal company and go home for a spell to visit her old sister in Edinburgh; so she was not present for the ceremonial occasion when King Tembinoka presented Louis before he sailed, and as a high sign of his regard,

the woven corselets of his grandfather, his father
and his uncle; odd souvenirs of Apemama, and
they must have been an awful nuisance to keep
on packing and carrying about.

His next letter to Colvin, quoted at the beginning of this chapter, was written at sea, 190 miles
off Samoa, on board the *Equator*. After Samoa, he
planned a passing visit to Fiji or Tonga, and then
home to England in June, by Sydney, Ceylon,
Suez and Marseilles. Of course all this while he
was writing up his South Seas notebook for the
editor who had first started him on these Pacific
cruises by commissioning a series of articles, and
he and Lloyd were also planning a full-length
yarn called *The Wrecker*.

When they were not running before a squall on
the *Equator*, they sat on deck in a dead calm,
suffering from the cruel heat, Louis very much
preferring the sort of weather that carried away
the fore-topmast. Finally they landed in Samoa,
and little-did-he-think that there half-way up a
mountain he would build himself a home to dwell
in for the rest of his life.

While they were in harbour, he stayed at Apia,
the capital, with an American trader. He reported that he used to write lying on the floor of

the back balcony, and the ink was dreadful, but the heat delicious, with a breeze stirring the palms, and for music the angry splash and roar of the Pacific on the reef—'where the warships are still piled from last year's hurricane'.

Although he thought the place less beautiful than the Marquesas or Tahiti, it cast a spell over him:

"I am now the owner of an estate upon Upolu, some two or three miles behind and above Apia; three streams, two waterfalls, a great cliff, an ancient native fort, a view of the sea and lowlands. . . . Besides all this, there is a great deal more forest than I have any need for; or to be plain the whole estate is one impassable jungle, which must be cut down and through at considerable expense. Then the house has to be built."

And joyfully he wrote to the doctor who used to look after him at Bournemouth, that he had now been for nearly two years in the South Seas, and was a person whom Dr. Scott would scarcely recognise:

"I think nothing of long walks and rides; I was four hours and a half gone the other day, partly riding, partly climbing up a steep ravine. I have stood a six months' voyage on a copra schooner with about three months ashore on coral atolls, which means (except for coconuts to drink) no change whatever from ship's food. My wife suffered badly—it was too rough a business altogether—Lloyd suffered—and, in short, I was the only one of the party who kept my end up."

So it is hardly surprising that their journey home to England that summer had been intended merely to see all his good friends again, wind up his affairs, and return in the autumn to settle in Samoa. Presently they found themselves on board the S.S. *Lübeck*, bound for Sydney. Three weeks later, Louis happened to pick up that newspaper in the Club which turned him from a man into a volcano; and the passion with which he wrote his Letter in Defence of Father Damien may have been responsible for another severe hæmorrhage from his lungs. He was so ill that the Australian doctors refused to let him quit the tropical climate. If he returned to Europe, they decreed, even for the summer months, he would surely die. So Louis and Lloyd and Fanny set off again on a trading schooner, the S.S. *Janet Nicholl*, a long low rakish craft painted black; she rolled terribly, and was known through the islands as the Jumping Jennie. They were only a rough day's journey out of Auckland when they were blown up by some materials for fireworks which had been stored in the main cabin—just the sort of thing, of course, that would happen to Stevenson, and leave him undaunted.

In November, 1890, they came again to Samoa. The house was to be built while Lloyd was sent back to England to bring out their own furniture. And Mrs. Stevenson serenely prepared to end her days in her son's home on a South Pacific island as soon as Vailima (which means Four Rivers) was ready to receive her.

Louis then developed one of his crazy enthusiasms over clearing and path-making and any sort of help he could give to his future garden and plantation, by swinging a hefty axe. His wife was probably kind enough not to remind him how he had once ruined the raspberry canes that were her pride and joy in their Bournemouth garden, by *pruning* them, as a delicious surprise for her while she was away on a visit for a couple of days;

he was no gardener, and pruning to him meant hacking. Those raspberry canes never bore fruit again! But preparation for the building of their house on Samoa needed no delicate fingers, and to hack away a jungle was more to Stevenson's taste; he had always enjoyed extremes:

". . . knife in hand, as long as my endurance lasted, I was to cut a path in the congested bush. At first it went ill with me; I got badly stung as high as the elbows by the stinging plant; I was nearly hung on a tough liana—a rotten trunk giving way under my feet. . . . Of a sudden things began to go strangely easier; I found stumps bushing out again; my body began to wonder, then my mind; I raised my eyes and looked ahead; and, by George, I was no longer pioneering, I had struck an old track overgrown, and was restoring an old path."

When Belle arrived, she was thrilled by her first sight of her new home, as they rode up the rocky path through a green tunnel with great trees meeting overhead, her horse giving little jumps over what she thought were streaks of fire on the ground till Louis explained it was phosphorus on bits of decayed wood. They turned out of the jungle forest on to the short road that led finally to the house, and she saw a densely wooded green mountain rise before her, with feathery fronds of coconut palms showing the height of the trees and frigate birds flying above; then, round another sharp turn, Vailima, a two-storey house painted bright blue with a red roof, and verandas upstairs and downstairs. They all sat for a little while resting on the veranda after their ride; over the tree-tops was a view of the Pacific spreading as far as the horizon, and Lloyd boasted: "There's nothing between us and the North Pole."

Soon Stevenson began speeding letters across the ocean, inviting all his friends to come out and stay and share his wild Paradise; his cousin, Graham Balfour, came and stayed a whole year. In the evenings, healthily tired out, he would tootle on the flageolet, till his family begged for mercy or shut themselves out of earshot; Stevenson adored music but he was no performer himself; and as none of the rest could play any instrument either, he had had to rely for years on the odd noises he managed to produce out of penny whistles. If only the gramophone, if only the radio had been invented during his lifetime, what heaven it would have brought him.

Still, he did not dwell too far from heaven at Vailima, once it was built. His native staff lovingly bestowed on him the Samoan name of Tusitala, which means 'teller of tales'. Fanny became Aolele, 'flying cloud', because of her constant activity about the house and estate, and Belle was Teuila (beautifying-the-ugly) when she too joined the Vailima group with her little boy Austin. R.L.S. always liked to have a boy around; and he gave Austin history lessons, but they left his junior with a rather one-sided and bewildered view of important events, because Louis believed that all of them had happened in Scotland.

There is a pack of fortune-telling cards called Teuila Cards, which have had a good sale for many years in the States; and it was Belle who originally planned and painted them while she was living in Samoa, in the intervals of her regular job of taking down her stepfather's books at dictation while he strode about the room. He had to dictate because by now he was a rueful victim of writer's cramp, and Belle was sure she could take down his books provided he helped her with the spelling, her weakest point (as Austin discovered when she tried to teach it to him!) She had a gift for painting, and she says that Stevenson was very interested and often used to come and watch her. From studying these cards, one can easily invent fragments of their conversation: "Oh Louis, *do* tell me how I'm to represent *Home* or *Calamity*, so that people see in a moment what each picture stands for?"—We can trace *Calamity*

straight back to Stevenson who might even have drawn it for her himself—he drew better than he played the flageolet!—because the little dancing devil hurling javelins was copied almost exactly from woodcuts of Apollyon in an old edition of

the *Pilgrim's Progress* quaintly illustrated by
Bagster, so often read to him, as a child, by
Cummy, his old nurse. He remembered the little
pictures vividly, and mentions them in one of his
essays, saying how Apollyon had terrified him. As
for *Home*, that card, too, he must have supplied: a
small fireplace of our old-fashioned kind, the kind

that smoked when there was an east wind blowing
down the chimney; Belle had never been to Scotland or England, so she must have been incredulous when he sketched it for her: "Look, Fanny,"
mischieviously, "what does this remind you of?"

134

and we can almost hear Fanny reply with a shudder: "The fireplace in Miss MacGregor's sitting-room at Braemar!" . . . Miss MacGregor's sitting-room at Braemar, and in the summer evenings of howling wind and rain, Uncle Tom and Aunt Maggie and Cousin Etta and Fanny and the little boy, Lloyd, collected round this smoky old fireplace, and Louis striding about the room, spinning the furniture round, while he read them the chapters he had just written of *Treasure Island*. . . .

One more picture from the *Teuila* pack of cards can be traced to Louis, not to Belle. The Wish Card. "Louis, how can I possibly *show* a Wish?" "By a ship in full sail," suggested the exile from

home. "A ship? But a ship isn't a Wish!" "Sometimes it can be."

But homesickness and the Wish Card were to come later; for the moment all was gas and gaiters at Vailima. And to his friends far away in Europe, fantastic legends began to drift in of how Tusitala lived in a palace like a king, beloved of dusky warriors. Pilgrims who revered his work travelled thousands of miles to visit him, and went away thrilled by his kindness and hospitality. Belle asked him whether fame was all it was cracked up to be, and after a moment's thought, Louis said smiling: "Yes, when I see my mother's face." The British warship *Curaçoa* was in harbour for a long while, and Louis and Lloyd and young Austin went aboard pretty often; while the steep path that struck off from the road across the island up to Vailima became known as 'the *Curaçoa* track', because it was worn down so often by the feet of the officers and men who were constantly visiting the Stevenson family; Louis remarked that their Commander treated him as if he were a slightly superior middy; and though by now he had grown to be a celebrity in a big way, his lack of self-importance made it still possible for one of the *Curaçoa's* midshipmen to exclaim in breathless astonishment to Belle, while looking at the books in the library at Vailima: "Good Lord, I never realised! *He's* the josser that wrote *Treasure Island*."

One day three horsemen came up to Vailima: two petty officers and a Corporal of Marines who addressed Stevenson thus: "Me and my shipmates inwites Mr. and Mrs. Stevens, Mrs. Strong, Mr. Austin and Mr. Balfour to a ball to be given to-night in the self-same 'all"; but usually 'Mr. Austin', who at the age of twelve had strong naval ambitions, was affectionately known among them all as 'The American Commodore':

"On Sunday, Austin and I went down to service and had lunch afterwards in the ward-room. The officers were awfully nice to Austin; they are the most amiable ship in the world; and after lunch we had a paper handed round on which we were to guess, and sign our guess, of the number of leaves on the pineapple; I never saw this game before, but it seems it is much practised in the Queen's Navee. When all have betted, one of the party begins to strip the pineapple head, and the person whose guess is furthest out has to pay for sherry. . . . I found that Austin had entered and lost about a bottle of sherry! He turned to me with great composure and addressed me: 'I am afraid I must look to you, Uncle Louis.' "

Austin was leading such a whale of a life that his relations decided it was getting a bit too much of a good thing:

"Louis pointed out that he was growing up like a little prince, which was true. The Samoans waited on him hand and foot; two able-bodied men would drop everything to lay out the tracks of his toy train; others would carry stones to help build his fort, and when he went into the forest to shoot pigeons a native boy walked behind him carrying his air gun."

—So they packed him off to school; first in California; but Belle was so miserable at the long distance stretching between them that afterwards they arranged instead for a school in Wellington, New Zealand, which (surprisingly to anyone bad at geography) is much nearer to Samoa. But during the long holidays:

"You must not suppose that Austin does nothing but build forts and walk among the woods and

swim in the rivers. On the contrary, he is sometimes a very busy and useful fellow . . . setting off
on horseback with his hand on his hip and his
pockets full of letters and orders, at the head of
quite a procession of huge white cart-horses with
pack-saddles, and big brown native men with
nothing on but gaudy kilts. Mighty well he
managed all his commissions; and those who saw
him ordering and eating his single-handed
luncheon in the queer little Chinese restaurant on
the beach declare he looked as if the place, and
the town, and the whole archipelago belonged to
him."

R.L.S. could always be amused by Austin's
exploits, and once wrote a poem for him to recite
to old Mrs. Stevenson on her birthday, which
brought in all the long words that could possibly
be fished up for the purpose:

Sole scholar of your college I appear.
Plenipotential for the party here
Assembled, elegantly to present
Their salutations and my compliment.

Awhile ago, when to your hands I came
I tripped on commas, stumbled at a name.

Browsed, like the sheep of some ungenerous
    breeder
On that lean pasture-land, a First Reader. . . .

Since when, a practised knight, fear laid aside,
Through verbal Alps, unfaltering I ride.
With polysyllables proved a passed practitioner,
And need not blush before a Land Commissioner.

We can imagine the happy grin with which he
listened to the lad's heroic effort to struggle
through to the end.

Austin, it might be out of revenge, then took to
writing stories himself, and the whole family
found it very difficult to keep solemn when he
read aloud the first, because he had heard how
R.L.S. had taken his friend W. E. Henley as
model for the voice and manners of Long John
Silver, and decided it would therefore be all right
to take his Uncle Lloyd as a model for his villain
'Mr. Morgan'; shortly before, his Uncle Lloyd
for some reason had refused to give him ten cents,
and Austin read out a little nervously: "Though
very handsome, Mr. Morgan was a miser."

Although R.L.S. had no sons or daughters of
his own, he was truly a Pied Piper and children

of all nations followed him round. He was, in fact, crazy on children, writing them long letters of gravest nonsense, or joining heart and soul in the games he invented for them, never too busy to stop and watch what they were up to:

"The children play marbles all along the street; and though they are generally very jolly, yet they get awfully cross over their marbles, and cry and fight like boys and girls at home. Another amusement in country places is to shoot fish with a bow and arrow. All round the beach there is bright shallow water where fishes can be seen darting or lying in shoals. The child trots round the shore, and wherever he sees a fish, lets fly an arrow and misses, and then wades in after his arrow. It is great fun (I have tried it) for the child, and I never heard of it doing any harm to the fishes. . . ."

He did not even mind being had by a child. There was once a pleasant little incident in Monterey where he was swindled by a small girl selling him a bucket of huckleberries falsely padded up with leaves underneath; after her remorseful confession, he remarked lightly to Fanny: "It's not bad sport to be a fool for five cents."

And children kept on coming into his life, more
boys than girls, though we have seen him play
croquet with the little leper girls in the Convent
garden at Molokai; but there had to be always a
boy knocking round; Lloyd first, of course, Lloyd
and *Treasure Island*, Lloyd and his toy printing-
press, Lloyd and the soldier games, racing with
Lloyd in canoes. When Lloyd grew up, Austin
replaced him, but Austin had a rival, Pola, a
faithful little native boy whom Belle first saw
standing 'erect in a gallant pose before the house,
leaning upon a long stick of sugar-cane, as though
it were a spear'. She wrote of him:

"Pola always spoke of Vailima as 'our place',
and of Stevenson as 'my chief'. I had given him
a pony that exactly matched his own skin. A
missionary meeting him in the forest road as he
was galloping along like a young centaur, asked:
'Who are you?' 'I,' answered Pola, reining in
with a gallant air, 'am one of the Vailima men!'
Pola bubbled over with fun, and his voice could
be heard chattering and singing gaily at any hour
of the day. He made up little verses about me,
which he sang to the graceful gestures of the siva
or native dance, showing unaffected delight when

commended. He cried out with joy and admiration when he first heard a hand-organ, and was excitedly happy when allowed to turn the handle. I gave him a box of tin soldiers, which he played with for hours in my room. He would arrange them on the floor, talking earnestly to himself in Samoan. 'These are brave brown men,' he would mutter. 'They are fighting for Mataafa. Boom! boom!' And with a wave of his arm he knocked down a whole battalion."

After Stevenson's death, Pola came to Belle and piteously begged for a 'sun-shadow of Tusitala, the beloved chief whom we all revere, but I more than the others, because he was the head of my clan'. So many mourners had already asked for photographs that she could only find one (from a weekly paper) which Louis himself had thought pretty awful, and he would have entirely agreed with the scornful way Pola threw it on the floor. "I will not have that!" he cried. "It is pig-faced. It is not the shadow of our chief!"—and suggested instead that he should be given a portrait of Stevenson hanging on the wall of the great hall. But Belle tenderly explained that this was impossible because it was by a very famous painter,

Sargent. Pola then demanded "that round one of tin"—a bronze medallion by a no less famous sculptor, and she could not help laughing at Pola's somewhat ambitious demands. Deeply hurt, he marched out. An hour or two later, she found the baby warrior, usually so proud of his dignity, lying face downwards on the veranda, crying bitterly: "I want the sun-shadow of Tusitala!" Belle's heart melted, and she gave him a good photograph—'which he wrapped in a banana-leaf, tying it carefully with a ribbon of grass'.

It would take far too long to describe how Stevenson was adored and revered by the natives, his own staff and the men of the different tribes, all of whom looked on him as a sort of king. Nor did he let it rest at picturesque pomp and panoply, but took a lot of trouble to make them see that not only must they not do certain things, but *why* they must not. When any of the staff were caught out in wrong-doing, he held a formal court of justice to make sure of the exact truth in the matter; and we have to hand it to him that anyhow in the following instance he had thought up an excellent punishment, not without humour, and certainly not without profit to the innocent:

144

"Fiaali'i, you have confessed that you stole the cooked pigs, the taro, the palusamis, the bread-fruit and the fish that fell to Vailima's portion at yesterday's feast. Your wish to eat was greater than your wish to be a gentleman. You have shown a bad heart and your sin is a great one, not alone for the pigs which count as naught, but because you have been false to your family. . . . It is easy to say that you are sorry, that you wish you were dead; but that is no answer. We have lost far more than a few dozen baskets of food; we have lost our trust in you. . . . You have hurt all our hearts here, not because of the pigs, but because we are ashamed and mortified before the world . . . if it reaches the ears of the great chiefs that treated us so handsomely, are we to say: 'Be not angry, gentlemen, four of our family are thieves; their respect and love for me is great, but their wish to eat pig is greater still'. . . . Fiaali'i, you are fined thirty dollars to be paid in weekly instalments. When the whole thirty dollars is ready it will be handed to you, and you will make us a great feast here in Vailima by way of atone-ment, and for every pig stolen there shall be two pigs, and for every taro, two taro, and so on and more also."

In Stevenson's letters to his friends about this strange life of his as an uncrowned king among natives, we always find a good deal about eating; for on an island where the inhabitants could not just run round to shops for whatever they wanted, the raising and getting of food (especially pigs) had a sort of solemn importance. An invitation to a feast presupposed a terrific affair. On one such occasion when the Vailima party were invited by Mataafa, the rebel king, to his small outlying island of Malie, they left home early in the morning, rode for miles down to the landing-pier, and then had a long journey in a canoe to Mataafa's village, where the presentations of food, apart from eating it, apparently took several hours, while a comic orator made his audience laugh by singing his announcements of the gifts: six thousand heads of taro, three hundred and nineteen cooked pigs—and a single turtle. Then Popo and his son, two of the most distinguished visitors, excepting of course Tusitala and his family, broke into a strange gambolling dance among the acres of cooked food, and *whatever they called for to leap over became theirs*, for that was the rule—(One cannot help wondering how this would work out, say, at a Lord Mayor's Banquet at the Guildhall?) One of Tusitala's biscuit-tins and a live calf were among the spoils they claimed, but most of the cooked food was given back again to the king, Mataafa. In spite of his modest refusal to dance and leap, Stevenson was presented with five live hens, four gourds of oil, four fine tapas, a hundred heads of taro, two cooked pigs, a cooked shark, two or three coconut branches strung with kava, *and* the turtle; a royal present for 'the white chief of the great powers'; then at a signal, a troup of young men with their lava-lavas like kilts, swooped down on the food field, and quickly gathered up the spoil into a separate pile for Stevenson to carry down to the boat when the feast was over: a cargo like the Swiss Family Robinson getting in provisions from the wreck. And the whole of the next morning R.L.S. was interrupted at his work by a solemn procession of men and women to inform him his turtle was now dead.

Any banquets given at Vailima for his native friends conformed to all the rites which the Samoans confidently expected from him; but when they were among themselves with only their own family and friends, they could, probably with relief, lapse into being natural, and enjoy themselves in their own way. Boredom was the only guest whom Louis would not for one moment allow inside his walls, and he was always thinking up something fresh when it struck him the house-party were getting dull and sitting round absorbed in their books. A merry old lady who as a young wife had lived at Apia with her husband in the Consular Service, remembers vividly the time when R.L.S. suggested that for a nice change they should each in turn invent and cook a main dish for every evening's meal, and no one else was to be let into the secret. He left his own turn till the very last, modestly vowing he hardly dared compete with the delicious surprises already cooked by the others . . . who might perhaps have noticed, if they had looked, a wicked gleam in his dark eyes. Gathered round the table in the big dining-hall, they all waited in a state of high expectancy. The door was flung open by two of the native boys, and Louis entered bearing triumphantly aloft a huge steaming dish, preceded by such a ghastly *smell* that none of them could stand it, and all rushed out, choking and protesting, into the open air. It was not just *a* smell, but all the horrible smells that ever were, brilliantly combined. . . . One of the times when admiration for the great writer might not have saved him from being murdered as a practical joker! But according to everyone who knew him personally, whatever trick he chose to play, he could somehow manage still to remain popular; a dangerous gift, only it happened to be allied with the kindest heart in the world, the bravest and the most generous.

In reading the Life—or rather the many Lives of R.L.S., one is liable to come to a full stop at a sentence like 'It is now necessary if we would understand a little of the Samoan wars, to give an idea of what were then the Government and politics of Samoa'. . . . And naturally we hope to skip several pages till we get to something interesting again. All the same, it will not be possible to understand why Stevenson suddenly found himself hotly involved in a war, unless we put up with just a quick layout of what were the existing 'Government and politics in Samoa': The island was governed by three nations in turn, Britain, Germany and the United States; the President and Chief Justice at that particular time were respectively a German and a Swede, and we had to keep our pledge to uphold them. The natives rebelled because their king, Mataafa, had been deposed in favour of a more pliant monarch, Malietoa, and they did not like his rule. While a warlike atmosphere menaced the island and before it actually broke out, Tusitala did his utmost in the cause of peace and fairness, at the risk of being deported by his enemies. This threat never actually materialised, though as usual he was officially in hot water all round, at home in England and with the existing government of Samoa, but we have noticed already how persuasive he could be as a champion of lost causes; Belle tells us that when their woods were full of scouting parties and they were continually interrupted by the beating of drums as warlike processions crossed the lawn, she once interrupted between two sentences of dictation: "Louis, have we a pistol or gun in the house that will *shoot*?" He answered with a careless "No, but we have friends on both sides", and went on cheerfully with his book. On land or at sea, travelling or lying in bed, nearly every moment of Stevenson's existence had been balanced on a knife-edge of safety; but this time it was slightly different; this at last was actual soldiering:

"Three hundred yards beyond is a second ford;

and there—I came face to face with war. Under the trees on the further bank sat a picket of seven men with Winchesters; their faces bright; their eyes ardent. As we came up, they did not speak or move; only their eyes followed us. The horses drank, and we passed the ford. . . . After dinner a messenger came up to me with a note, that the wounded were arriving at the Mission House. Fanny, Lloyd and I saddled and rode off with a lantern."

His personal sympathies were passionately with Mataafa; and grief at his hero's defeat found vent in one of his uncontrollable bursts of justifiable anger at the way Mataafa's supporters were being treated in prison at Apia. He went down to the noisy jail, laden with food for the starving prisoners; paid a doctor to attend to their wounds after they had been flogged through the streets, and helped in cleaning out the filthy prison . . . which so shamed the officials that they themselves took action in the matter.

When the year of imprisonment was over, eight of the chiefs went up in a deputation to Vailima, where they squatted in a semi-circle with Tusitala and his family, and drank 'ava', and made formal speeches of gratitude for every kindness he had ever shown them. Speeches, of course, are always easy, but they went on with an offer to make a road sixty feet wide connecting Vailima with the main highroad across the island; up till now, there had been no more than a path winding up through a dense jungle of immense trees. The Samoans detested manual work; road-making in particular was felt to be degrading to warriors; and they had not yet been back to their own homes to see their families and cope with their deserted lands; also they were deeply impoverished, but insisted nevertheless on paying for all the necessary material and maintenance during its building. A bluff English sea-captain happened to ride by and saw Mataafa's chiefs laughing and singing at their work; he leapt from his horse and exclaiming: "I must be in on this!" seized an axe and swung it at the highest tree.

R.L.S. had tried in vain to refuse; and when they wished to name it 'The Road of the Loving Heart' he said it should be known instead as the Road of Gratitude. When it was eventually declared open, the chiefs desired all their names and titles to be painted on a board set up at the cross-roads, with this inscription:

Considering the great love of Tusitala in his loving care of us in our distress in the prison, we have therefore prepared a splendid gift. It shall never be muddy, it shall endure for ever, this road that we have dug.

CHAPTER SEVEN

A FAMOUS Yorkshire cricketer was once quoted as saying: "I was always happy as long as I was bowling," and Andrew Lang added to this that he thought Stevenson was almost always happy when he was writing. Even lying flat in bed, not allowed to speak for fear of starting another hæmorrhage, he learnt the Deaf and Dumb language, and Belle learnt it too, so that he could go on dictating to her. So all through these active, restless, changing years, you can imagine him continuing to pour out an amazing quantity of books; the uniform editions published since his death will fill several shelves; and if we stand in front of them remembering that he only lived till he was forty-four, and that many weeks and months of every year were spent in being dangerously ill, remembering also that he was no careless writer, but went over every word again and again, intent on making it quite right for the reader as well as for his own satisfaction, we may wonder how he managed to achieve so much? Titles leap out at us familiar as *Treasure Island*, *Kidnapped*, *Jekyll and Hyde*; volumes of treasure for all who care to delve for it; a treasure-hunter himself, as we know, the very word fascinated him— (if you look up *treasure-trove* in the dictionary, you will find that it means 'gold hidden in the earth, of unknown ownership'). Yet by one long delightful story called *The Treasure of Franchard* he revealed how in his soul he was nevertheless sharply aware that the human side of life must never be sacrificed to a treasure-trove of 'doubloons and double guineas and moidores and sequins', of 'gold, flagons, and candlesticks, encrusted with the earth of ages'. And the treasure in *The Wrecker* had a curse on it; one can hardly think without horror of what was done aboard the *Flying Scud* by the crew of the *Currency Lass*:

. . . the inestimable treasure chest slung upon two oars . . . conspicuous in the shining of the fire.

"There's my beauty!" cried Wicks, viewing it with a cocked head; "that's better than a bonfire. What! we have a chest here, and bills for close upon two thousand pounds; there's no show to that—it would go in your vest-pocket—but the rest! upwards of forty pounds avoirdupois of coined gold, and close on two hundred-weight of Chile silver! What! ain't that good enough to fetch a fleet? Do you mean to say that won't affect a ship's compass? Do you mean to tell me that the look-out won't turn to and smell it?" he cried.

Mac, who had no part nor lot in the bills, the forty pounds of gold, or the two hundredweight of silver, heard this with impatience, and fell into a bitter choking laughter. "You'll see!" he said harshly. "You'll be glad to feed them bills into the fire before you're through with it!"

'The Bottle Imp', one of three stories in a volume of *Island Nights' Entertainments*, works up to present the same warning as his other treasure stories; but unlike the others, it has a happy ending. Stevenson himself liked it well; pleased that it should have been actually translated into Samoan, the first serial ever read by Samoans in their own language, with wonder and delight. It never occurred to their simplicity that every word Tusitala chose to set down was not actual and factual truth. "They do not know what it is to make up a story," and he relates how little groups of Samoans used to go up to visit Vailima, pretend to admire everything they saw, the furniture, pictures, curios and so forth, but at the end of their visit, getting more and more uneasy when their host failed to produce what they had really come up to see, burst out at last with *"Where is the bottle?"*

Nearly every author has certain themes on his mind, besides what is in it. Treasure and islands and quarrels, these for some reason keep on recurring in nearly everything R.L.S. ever wrote. There is a chapter in *Kidnapped* called 'The Quarrel', when Alan Breck and David Balfour, in their flight across the heather from the King's men, come near to killing one another; anger is a solid barrier between them . . . the unbearable tension at last snaps . . . and David draws sword upon Alan Breck Stewart:

". . . I am no blower and boaster like some that I could name. Come on!" And drawing my sword, I fell on guard as Alan himself had taught me.

"David!" he cried. "Are ye daft? I cannae draw upon ye, David. It's fair murder."

"That was your look-out when you insulted me," said I.

157

"It's the truth!" cried Alan, and he stood for a moment, wringing his mouth in his hand like a man in sore perplexity. "It's the bare truth," he said, and drew his sword. But before I could touch his blade with mine, he had thrown it from him and fallen to the ground. "Na, na," he kept saying, "na, na—I cannae, I cannae."

At this the last of my anger oozed all out of me; and I found myself only sick, and sorry, and blank, and wondering at myself. I would have given the world to take back what I had said; but a word once spoken, who can recapture it? I minded me of all Alan's kindness and courage in the past, how he had helped and cheered and borne with me in our evil days; and then recalled my own insults, and saw that I had lost for ever that doughty friend. At the same time, the sickness that hung upon me seemed to redouble, and the pang in my side was like a sword for sharpness. I thought I must have swooned where I stood.

This it was that gave me a thought. No apology could blot out what I had said; it was needless to think of one, none could cover the offence; but where an apology was vain, a mere cry for help might bring Alan back to my side. I put my pride away from me. "Alan!" I said; "if you cannae help me, I must just die here."

And that was the end of trouble, for both were noble-hearted men.

The duel between the brothers in *The Master of Ballantrae* was a different matter, for the elder brother, the exile James Durie, was the devil himself:

". . . there was no breath stirring; a windless stricture of frost had bound the air; and as we went forth in the shine of the candles, the blackness was like a roof over our heads. Never a word was said; there was never a sound but the creaking of our steps along the frozen path. The cold of the night fell about me like a bucket of water; I shook as I went with more than terror; but my companions, bare-headed like myself, and fresh from the warm hall, appeared not even conscious of the change.

'Here is the place,' said the Master. 'Set down the candles.'

I did as he bid me, and presently the flames went up, as steady as in a chamber, in the midst of the frosted trees and I beheld these two brothers take their places. . . . Mr. Henry took and kept the upper hand from the engagement, crowding in upon his foe with a contained and glowing fury. Nearer and nearer he crept upon the man, till of a sudden the Master leaped back with a little sobbing oath; and I believe the movement brought the light once more against his eyes. To it they went again, on the fresh ground; but now methought closer, Mr. Henry pressing more outrageously, the Master beyond doubt with shaken confidence. For it is beyond doubt he now recognised himself for lost, and had some taste of the cold agony of fear; or he had never attempted the foul stroke. I cannot say I followed it, my untrained eye was never quick enough to seize details, but it appears he caught his brother's blade with his left hand, a practice not permitted. Certainly Mr. Henry only saved himself by leaping on one side; as certainly the Master, lunging in the air, stumbled on his knee, and before he could move the sword was through his body.

I cried out with a stifled scream, and ran in; but the body was already fallen to the ground, where it writhed a moment like a trodden worm, and then lay motionless."

If *The Master of Ballantrae* was grim enough, *The Wrecker* and *The Ebb-Tide*, written in collaboration with Lloyd, showed Stevenson in an even darker mood. One could hardly believe they were bitten out by the same author as the rollicking thriller they had invented: *The Wrong Box*. What had gone amiss with him? His actual power to write grew stronger and stronger, but after *The Ebb-Tide* he simply could not find a subject to suit him. One idea after another he picked up with enthusiasm, wrote home that he was well away with it, and then impatiently chucked it again. It may have been chiefly the titles that seduced him; Heathercat, The Great North Road, The Young Chevalier, The Shovels of Newton French, Dyce of Ythan, Sofia Scarlet. After beginning a book called *The Justice Clerk*, R.L.S. abandoned it and settled down to *St. Ives*; both stories were laid in Edinburgh and the Pentlands, his 'hills of home'. . . . Yes, the man was homesick ('A ship isn't a Wish' 'Sometimes it is!') Even the strident tropical rains, drawing near across the forest and bursting on his roof, reminded him of Scotland too poignantly for comfort:

"All the smells of the good wet earth, sweetly,

M

with a kind of Highland touch; the crystal rods of the shower, as I look up, have drawn their criss-cross over everything; and a gentle and very welcome coolness comes up around me in little draughts, blessed draughts. . . ."

We can gather he was homesick from nearly all his letters, and especially those to his pen-friend and fellow-countryman, a certain J. M. Barrie, who one day was to write *Peter Pan*. Barrie had been a solemn industrious student of Edinburgh University, and remained solemn and industrious and a bit of a prig for some time afterwards; in an essay reminiscing on other earlier students more idle and profligate than himself, he condemned Robert Louis Stevenson for writing too lightly and flippantly and not always as well as undoubtedly he could; he had better therefore pull up his socks (or the Scottish equivalent for pulling them up) and try and do better. Stevenson happened to re-read this essay, and in a letter flushed with warm admiration for Barrie's book *A Window in Thrums*, he mentioned the scolding he had received, and added: 'I have half a mind to give you back some of your own sauce and see how you like it!' On receiving such a generous letter, Barrie was completely conquered, and Stevenson became his hero; they carried on with the correspondence . . . and R.L.S. was convinced that years ago when he was unsuccessfully fishing a trout stream not far from Kirriemuir, Barrie had been the small boy who came along and spoke to him. He was continually pressing the younger writer to come out and stay with him at Vailima, and Barrie longed to do so; only his mother begged him pathetically to wait till she was dead; for she was terribly jealous of the more mature man whose genius was a challenge to that of her precious Jamie; and to the latter's great amusement, always pretended Stevenson's heart was black and his books unreadable; she would not touch them with a barge pole! She called him 'that Stevenson man', and if her son so much as mentioned the aggravating name, she would reply with a stiff "Oh?" Barrie must have betrayed her in his letters to R.L.S., who delighted in her bad opinion of him. "The scoundrel," she once said, "I could never thole his books"; her son reminded her that she had never read any of them; "And never will," she replied with spirit. Barrie went on to relate with twinkling eyes how he would put the *Master of Ballantrae* in his mother's way on purpose, leaving it on the table beside her bed, or going so far as to hide her spectacles in it or prop it up against her teapot. And once, looking through a keyhole, he saw her so wrapped up in that very book that he bounced in hoping to catch her at it, but she was too quick and was gazing out of the window. . . .

" 'You have been sitting very quietly, mother.'

'I always sit quietly, I never do anything, I'm just a finished stocking.'

'Have you been reading?'

'Do I ever read at this time of the day?'

'What is that in your lap?'

'Just my apron.'

'Is that a book beneath the apron?'

'It might be a book.'

'Let me see.'

'Go away with you to your work.'

But I lifted the apron. 'Why, it's *The Master of Ballantrae*!' I exclaimed, shocked.

'So it is!' said my mother, equally surprised. But I looked sternly at her, and perhaps she blushed.

'Well, what do you think: not nearly equal to mine?' said I with humour.

'Nothing like them,' she said determinedly."

All the same, the game went on, and the next time they had some such passage of arms was over *Treasure Island*, which she read openly this time, anxiously assuring Jamie that it was just to make certain it was not as good as any *he* had written . . . (but when he put his hands over her eyes that she might know he had come into the room, she tried to read the book between his fingers!)— "Those pirate stories are so uninteresting," Jamie would remark gravely; "do you think you will finish this one?" "I may as well go on with it since I have begun it." "There are none of those one-legged scoundrels in my books," he would say. "Better without them," she replied promptly, and then, with an anxious look: "You surely believe I like yours best?" Yet she read *Treasure Island*—

". . . holding it close to the ribs of the fire because she could not spare a moment to rise and light the gas), and when bed-time came, and we coaxed, remonstrated, scolded, she said quite fiercely, clinging to the book: 'I dinna lay my head on a pillow this night till I see how that laddie got out of the barrel.' "

And still Barrie longed to go out to Vailima . . .
until the bad news came which put an end to all
thoughts of such a trip:

"I shall never go up the Road of Loving Hearts
now, on a wonderful clear night of stars, to meet
the man coming towards me on a horse. It is still
a wonderful clear night of stars, but the road is
empty. So I never saw the dear king of us all.
But before he had written books, he was in my
part of the country with a fishing-wand in his
hand, and I like to think that I was the boy who
met him that day by Queen Margaret's burn,
where the rowans are, and busked a fly for him,
and stood watching, while his lithe figure rose and
fell as he cast and hinted back from the crystal
waters of Noran-side."

Louis stayed on in the South Pacific, making no
useless attempt to reverse the verdict of the doctors
who went on steadily saying that whereas now he
was well, any climate not of the tropics would
finish him off quickly. He wrote to his cousin Bob:

"I have so huge a desire to know exactly what
you are doing, that I suppose I should tell you

what I am doing by way of an example. I have a room now, a part of the twelve-foot veranda sparred in, at the most inaccessible end of the house. Daily I see the sunrise out of my bed, which I still value as a tonic, a perpetual tuning fork, a look of God's face once in the day. At six my breakfast comes up to me here, and I work till eleven. If I am quite well, I sometimes go out and bathe in the river before lunch, twelve. In the afternoon I generally work again, now alone drafting, now with Belle dictating. Dinner is at six, and I am often in bed by eight. This is supposing me to stay at home. But I must often be away, sometimes all day long, sometimes till twelve, one, or two at night, when you might see me coming home to the sleeping house, sometimes in a trackless darkness, sometimes with a glorious tropic moon, everything drenched with dew— unsaddling and creeping to bed; and you would no longer be surprised that I live out in this country, and not in Bournemouth—in bed."

Yet he was thoroughly dissatisfied with the work of a lifetime: "I ought to have been able to build lighthouses and write too." It was strange he should have felt so discouraged, because his fame was swelling with every book, and it was during this spring of 1894 that his old friends wrote him from home that they were bringing out a handsome uniform edition of his works, the Edinburgh Edition. And at the news he did another incredulous burst of little-did-I-think, reminding Charles Baxter, from whom he first heard about the project, of those early days together when they used to search their pockets for coppers, very often without success, to produce three halfpennies necessary for two glasses of beer in the Lothian Road.

The first eight months of that year were spent dictating *St. Ives*, rather slowly and painfully; it was never one of his favourites:

"I'm as sick of the thing as ever anyone can be; it's a rudderless hulk; it's a pagoda, and you can just feel—or I can feel—that it might have been a pleasant story, if it had been only blessed at baptism."

And then within a few chapters of the end, he suddenly threw it up and went back to *The Justice Clerk*, re-named *Weir of Hermiston*. Belle reported that the pace of Louis' dictation was now quite amazing; he would stride about the room pouring it out, never hesitating for a word, as though he had it all in front of him. The first time when, according to custom, he read aloud to his family in the evening what he had done during the day, Lloyd was so overwhelmed by its strength and power, that while the others praised and prophesied success, he sat silent, unable to find words. Still in silence, he was just going off to bed when Louis called him back; and to his amazement, it was Louis in a passion over Lloyd thinking the story so bad that he could not find one single thing to say in its favour. Lloyd had quite a job to convince him to the contrary!

Weir of Hermiston was far and away the best book R.L.S. ever wrote; and yet for the most tragic reason of all, we can hardly call it a book, only a fragment. A very good writer called Quiller-Couch ('Q' was the name he wrote under) was to finish *St. Ives*, but no one dared touch *Weir of Hermiston*—a masterpiece could only be handled by its master.

Towards sunset of December 3rd, feeling thoroughly happy and wonderfully well after a good morning's dictation, he joined Fanny to show her, as he always did, the chapter he was half-way through, to make sure that she approved. He found her, however, in a queer depressed mood; so to cheer her up, he played a game of cards with her, mentioned hopefully a lecture-tour in America that he felt he was quite well enough to undertake, and then, as she remained still melancholy, went down to the cellar to fetch up a special bottle of Burgundy, as he said they would celebrate the evening with a little feast and he himself would mix the salad—he had a gift for salads. Talking away in the same eager vein, he suddenly put both hands to his head and cried out sharply: "What's that?"—then fell unconscious on the veranda.

They carried him into the great hall; and he died a couple of hours later, in the arm-chair which had once been his grandfather's, and which Lloyd had brought out from their old home in Edinburgh.

Members of his household who loved to call themselves the Clan Tusitala, knelt round the couch where he lay wrapped in the Union Jack which had flown above Vailima, praying in Latin and Samoan; veterans of native tribes filed past his body, bringing their most precious finely-woven mats that had been in their families for many generations, and laying them over him so that the Union Jack could hardly be seen: "Talofa Tusitala!" they murmured reverently. One of Mataafa's old Chiefs who had helped build The Road of the Loving Hearts, spoke sorrowfully for them all.

"Sleep, Tusitala! I am poor, and can give nothing this last day he receives his friends. Yet I am not afraid to come and look the last time in my friend's face, never to see him more till we meet with God. Behold! Tusitala is dead; Mataafa is also dead to us. These two great friends have been taken by God. When Mataafa was taken, who was our support but Tusitala? We were in prison, and he cared for us. We were sick, and he made us well. We were hungry, and he fed us. The day was no longer than his kindness."

Lloyd remembered now how Stevenson had often remarked that he would like to be buried on the very top of Mount Vaea. There was no way up through the impenetrable tangle of scrub and undergrowth, so he summoned the younger and stronger of the tribesmen from all over the island,

and with the first light of dawn they began to hew a track up the steep slope to the summit. By noon it was done; the ensign of the *Casco* was laid over the bier which was carried shoulder-high by tall dusky warriors; and followed by a long procession of mourners, nearly every inhabitant of the island, brown and white and of all nationalities, trudging in the blazing heat up the path to the narrow ledge at the top. After a brief burial service, an ancient chieftain stepped forward and announced that henceforth no firearms were ever to be used on the mountain, so that the birds which Tusitala loved to hear, might still, and without fear, sing round his grave.

This was the sort of tribute to have made Stevenson glad. And from a thousand others which reached his family after his death, we can pick out an odd two or three to stand for the rest. For instance, the three lines Fanny received saying: 'Dear Madam—All over the world people will be sorry for the death of Robert Louis Stevenson, but none will mourn him more than the blind white leper at Molokai.' Or that incident with the flavour of a sad little fairy-tale, telling how Fanny and Belle left Vailima after Louis' death, trying to get away from their grief; and then, without announcing it, came back from their travels a year later to see if they could after all bear to live there without him. As nobody was expecting them, the house was deserted and must have seemed terribly empty and forlorn. Too weary to send out word to their former staff that they had arrived, they decided it could wait till the next day, and went wearily to bed. Belle slept late, tired from her journey; sprang up guiltily when she woke, and ran to the window. . . . Then stood amazed at what she saw:

"Smoke coming out of the cook-house chimney, Talolo at the door, and Lopu, the yard man, coming up with a pail of water—all the business of the place, in fact, going on like clockwork, just as though they had never been absent for a day! Running into her mother's room, she found her sitting up in bed just finishing her breakfast, which had been brought up on a tray by Sosimo. The news had gone forth the night before that they had returned, and every man of the Vailima force was at his post at break of day."

And a story which happened at the Stevenson Memorial Meeting in Edinburgh: His mother had said beforehand that she would not sit on the platform, because she had an old-fashioned idea that platforms were proper only for men; but by the time she arrived at the main entrance with her ticket for a reserved seat in the body of the hall, such a surging crowd was clamouring to be admitted, that she was afraid of being turned away. So she appealed to a policeman to get her in:

"It's nae use, it's fu'," he said; "reserve seats ta'en an hour ago by folks that had nae tuckets, and they would na gang out."

"I must get in," cried Mrs. Stevenson, roused out of her usual calm by despair. "I've a right to get in. I am Robert Louis Stevenson's mother."

"Aye, you've the best right," the policeman replied, and, turning to the crowd, cried: "Mak' way there. She maun get in. She's Roabert Louis's mither."

People who thought themselves packed too tightly to move somehow packed closer, and let Mrs. Stevenson squeeze and wriggle past. Breathless, hustled, and, for once, her mantle and bonnet a little awry, much against her will the crowd pushed her on to the platform.

Hiding herself as far back as she could, from there she heard a magnificent speech about her son, matching the epitaph spoken by Mataafa's old warrior. . . . "Because of him," said J. M. Barrie, "the most worthy of us were more worthy and the meanest of us a little less mean."

And here is the last item for our small strange collection of tributes which we have invisibly labelled 'little-did-I-think': two packets of stamps, one set issued in 1935, the other in 1939. Among the former is a picture of Vailima, and another has a picture of the burial-place of R.L.S. on the crest of the mountain; in 1939, the head of Stevenson himself was chosen for one of a somewhat rarer issue of only four stamps, commemorating the 25th anniversary of the Australians landing on the island and taking possession of it at the outbreak of the 1914–1918 war. Belle once described the excitement there used to be whenever the mail came in and they stopped work for the day:

". . . We have to wait our turn as Louis throws them out . . . he gives Austin all the picture-papers to open, and as he looks over his own letters he gives me those from strangers and autograph collectors. '. . . Sir, I think you are the greatest author living. Please send me a complete set of Samoan stamps!' "

So this stamp in particular would probably have made him laugh a lot, because he never thought he was the 'greatest author living', nor indeed that he would be remembered and honoured sixty years after he was dead, as we remember and honour him now.